AF541756

HAZARDOUS WASTE MANAGEMENT

DPH Management Series

HAZARDOUS WASTE MANAGEMENT

J M DEWAN • K NSUDARSHAN

DISCOVERY PUBLISHING HOUSE
NEW DELHI-110002

Discovery Publishing House
4831/24, Ansari Road, Darya Ganj
New Delhi - 110 002 (INDIA)

Hazardous Waste Management

Reprinted-2011
ISBN-81-7141-351-x

PRINTED IN INDIA

Printed at Mehra Offset Press, Delhi

Preface

The management world is in transition. The causes of this transition are many, but the major one is the vast changes in knowledge and in the information that flows in and out of organizations. This changing information disrupts traditions, established processes, well-known procedures, and routine ways of doing things. New principles, concepts, techniques, ideas, expressions, processes, and procedures are emerging, moving us to a new plateau of professional practice. Trying to capture this changing knowledge and information is like trying to capture the atmosphere. How can you do it when the atmosphere is continually shifting and when you need the atmosphere to do the capturing? The best we can do is find a peak from which we can at least get a perspective on management as a whole, decide on the work and responsibilities of management, and gather in whatever practical management information we can. A team of experts in this series represent some of the best contemporary thinking and information available. They represent many major successful corporations, active consulting agencies, and well-known educational institutions, and all are experts on what is happening with the flow of knowledge and information in the management world. This is a lofty pinnacle from which to survey the management world.

Managers and supervisors clamor for current information and guidelines to help solve formidable problems in their work world—problems that range from "how to do it" to "how to resolve conflict when doing it." Many problems are generated from miscommunication and incompetence. As the management practice proceeds from the complex to the supercomplex, problem solving becomes a large-scale challenge requiring new knowledge and skills. Managers and supervisors cannot wait for research breakthroughs with real-world answers to solve these dilemmas. They must tackle them here and now with the useful information and proven practices immediately available. Whether making a decision, solving a problem setting up a procedure, designing a process, or resolving a behaviour conflict, a manager must rely heavily on information. To a great extent, management practitioners are information workers; that is, they generate, distribute, store, retrieve, and consume information. Competence in finding and using the right information at the needed time determines to a considerable extent competence in the management function, activity, or responsibility. The *DPH Management Series* attempts to fill this need for usable information in spite of the changing nature of its subject.

The *DPH Management Series* not a book to be read and later discarded. It is a reference book, a tool to be used by managerial personnel in the day-to-day work of an organization. Like a tool, it should never be more than a reach away when a new situation emerges that demands its use. This series aim to achieve a first-and practical and proven knowledge and information as a self-development opportunity for those who are moving into or upward in management. A complete spectrum of management subjects is immediately available for orientation, study, analysis, assimilation, and problem solving. Within one set of covers is the view of management as a totality. The management field is loaded with ideas that the organization of this handbook series unique logic. It follows both levels and areas of responsibilities of an organization.

The work of this handbook series is the collaborative effort of many outstanding people in the management field. The motivation for this work varied from individual to individual, but the central motivation that united us all was the excitement of capturing the management state-of-the-art and sharing it with colleagues in the dynamic profession of management.

This series should be of great help to managerial practitioners at any organizational level who are responsible for a function, department, or set of responsibilities. The handbook series will also give these practitioners insights into management roles and approaches in other areas as well. The subject matter encompasses top, middle, and lower management. Special emphasis was placed on managing people, time, space, budgets, and resources to give the handbook extra utility for middle and lower management. Students of management in university or educational institutions will find the series an invaluable resource for adding "real world" practices to their academic and theoretical foundations. MBA students will gain an invaluable overview of the total organization to complement their MBA degree. Administrators and public managers can become acquainted with practices employed by managers and supervisors in private organizations. These practices are not always directly applicable in public sector bodies, but with thought and modifications, these private practices can adapt to public organizations. Public and university librarians will find the handbook an indispensable reference for the multitude of questions on many topics from the general public, special groups, associations, and students.

Editors

Contents

1 Hazardous Wastes

Hazardous wastes are approximately 1% of the total U.S. solid waste stream. Despite this low percentage, the generation, storage, treatment, disposal, and transportation of hazardous wastes have developed into an entire business sector that materially and financially affects both government and the private sector. This chapter focuses on an analysis of th major U.S. waste laws affecting environmental practice.

The owner or operator of a facility that produces a raw material or manufactures products, by-products, and intermediate goods is responsible for the association generation of wastes and pollutants from facility activities. The laws and regulations in this country hold owners/ operators of wastes and pollutants responsible for ultimate disposition of these materials. Therefore, to owners/operators or employees, the procedures and methods involved in disposition of wastes and pollutants are critical to the survival of their business.

Public perception alone, even if not correct in the assessment of responsibility for wastes and pollutants, can also influence the survival and economics of a business; therefore, it is essential for environmental decision making to occur responsibly. The decisions made on the wastes and pollutants generated and ultimate disposition of materials-disposal, treatment, recycling, or reuse-are as important as the decisions of what materials, goods, or products a business is providing to the customers.

Environmental laws and regulations in recent years are focusing on where wastes and pollutants are generated and methods to reduce them. Regulatory agencies are examining multimedia in attempts to reduce use of the most toxic chemicals. Pollutants existing stacks or popes may originate from a different medium.

Worldwide, there is clear regulatory movement away from treatment, storage, and disposal of wastes and toward prevention and minimization. However, in order to understand the existing U.S. regulatory framework governing hazardous wastes, several concepts and definitions must be clearly understood. Often the practical uses of term differ from the regulatory definition. It is the regulatory definition that subjects a facility owner/operator or custodian to the requirements of a law or regulatory program. Therefore, understanding the regulatory terms and definitions is a key in the development of environmental management programs and implementation of environmental practices.

As of this writing, *solid waste* means solid,

liquid, semisolid, and gaseous material which is discarded or meant for discard. The waste must be a solid waste by definition to qualify as a hazardous waste.

The distinction of a *waste* and a *product* is an important one in the regulations. This can be illustrated by the distinction of the chemical products stored in a tank versus the same material leaking from the tank. For example, if the tank leaks and contaminates soil, a solid waste is produced when the material is disposed. Thus, the "product" chemical in the tank has now become a "waste"—intended for discard unless it could be reused or recycled as an ingredient in another process.

There is also a distinction between a hazardous *waste* and a hazardous *substance*. The RCRA regulations define *hazardous waste* in two distinct categories; listed hazardous waste and characteristic hazardous waste. Wastes may be identified in these categories by process knowledge.

The categories of hazardous waste are more narrowly defined than the categories of hazardous substances. A hazardous substance cab be a wastes well as a commercial product. Many of the chemicals considered hazardous substances are ingredients in making a product or intermediate product. The regulatory road is complex and begins in tracking a chemical from the time it is received at a facility through storage, use, and any residue and/or waste produced from use to its ultimate disposition.

The help readers negotiate the convoluted regulatory road, this chapter is organized to systematically review and discuss major U.S. waste laws. The intent of this discussion is to provide a stand-along analysis of the following topics and laws:

- Solid and hazardous wastes under the Resource Conservation Recovery Act as amended. This discussion includes underground storage tank rules and land disposal requirements under the Hazardous and Solid Waste Amendments of 1984. The HSWA is a revision to the RCRA statues. The section also covers management of hazardous substances in above ground storage tanks as well as management of hazardous substances during transporation. Transportation of hazardous substances is also regulated by the Hazardous Materials Transportation Act, Department Air Transport association Shipping Requirements.
- Polychlorinated biphenyl storage, disposal, and cleanup requirements.
- Water quality issues under the Clear Water Act Discharge Elimination System .
- Air quality issues under the Clean Air Act of 1990 .
- Comprehensive Environmental Response, Compensation and Liability Act also known as Superfund.

- Spill assessment and response under CERCLA.
- Emergency Planning and Community Right to Know Act.
- Regulated medical waste-Medical Waste Tracking Act of 1988.
- Radioactive and mixed wastes.

Due to the ever-changing nature of the state and federal regulatory environment, the subsequent discussions must be viewed as general reviews and not as specific compliance manuals. Appropriate legal and/or regulatory compliance guidance should be obtained as needed.

Solid and hazardous wastes: RCRA

The hazardous waste issue is not new, despite the widespread public perception that hazardous materials problems began with the 1977 Love Canal episode. In fact, industrial activity and its waste by products are not the only sources of hazardous waste. There are six primary producers of hazardous waste.

- industrial : manufacturing and formulating processes, oil, gas, and mining
- municipal; power generation facilities and waste treatment facilities
- hospital: biomedical and infectious
- decommissioning: land and buildings
- nuclear
- agricultural.

In the United States, *hazardous waste* has a specific regulatory definition developed by Congress in the passages of RCRA on October 21, 1976;

> Hazardous waste is (a) solid waste, or a combination of solid wastes which because of its quantity, concentration, or physical chemical or infectious characteristics may (b) pose a substantial present or potential hazard... when improperly treated, stored, transported, or disposed of, otherwise managed.

The RCRA was developed in order to provide a national framework for waste management, and its scope includes solid, liquid, and gas. The U.S. EPA stated, "A fundamental premise of the statute is that human health and the environment will best be protected by careful management of the transportation, treatment, storage, and disposal of hazardous waste, in accordance with standards developed under the Act " The clear thrust of the EPA' s statement is to create a cradle-to-grave regulatory system.

The RCRA, as an amendment to the Solid Waste Disposal Act, governs solid and hazardous waste management. The RCRA was enacted in 1976 and amended in 1984. The object of this legislation is to regulate both municipal and hazardous waste disposal and to encourage resource recovery and recycling. Most of the regulations developed under the RCRA concern the control of hazardous waste generators, transporters, and treatment, storage, and disposal facilities. The RCRA authorizes the EPA to list materials as hazardous wastes and to develop a management system from cradle to grave. This management system includes record keeping, labeling, and handling requirements for these wastes.

The Hazardous Materials Transportation Act, referenced by the RCRA, provides for the regulation of hazardous materials that are transported by air, water, rail, or highway. It authorizes the U.S. Department of Transportation to issue requirements for the packaging, labeling, and transport of all hazardous materials shipments. The HMTA expands the regulated system to include materials as well as wastes. Thus, products are regulated as well as hazardous wastes.

RCRA waste materials: Characteristics

Regulation require that all wastes be classified as hazardous or nonhazardous before their storage, treatment, or disposal. As a general rule, wastes can not leave a given facility before the characterization of their hazardous nature. The following are questions that must be addressed in order to determine which type of waste material has been generated:

1. Is the waste material excluded from regulation?
2. Is the waste material a listed waste?
3. Does the waste material exhibit any of the following hazardous characteristics:

- Ignitability (I)- liquid with a flash point of less than 140 F
- Corrosivity-pH less than or equal to 2 or pH greater than or equal to 12.5
- Reactivity-sulfur- or cyanide-bearing wastes or normally unstable or capable of detonating at standard temperature and pressure
- TCLP toxicity-organic, metal, or pesticide-bearing wastes.

The generator characterizes each waste stream based on the above criteria and generator knowledge of the process from which waste is generated. The generator must conduct sampling and analysis of wastes if changes in a waste stream occur or if the generator is unsure of the characteristics or components of the waste.

Characteristic wastes are on longer considered hazardous if on-site treatment eliminates the hazardous characteristics. Neutralization of acid wastewater in the acid waste storage tank is a good example of a corrosive waste made nonhazardous through treatment.

RCRA: EPA Generator requirements

A *Generator* is defined as a person, by site, whose act or process produces hazardous waste. A generator of hazardous waste must not treat, store, dispose of, transport, or offer for transportation, hazardous waste without having received an EPA identification number. A generator must not offer hazardous waste to transporters or to treatment, storage, or disposal facilities that have not received an EPA identification number. The following delineates the federal requirements; some states have more stringent generator requirements.

Generator categories. A generator's status and specific requirements may change from month to month, depending on chemicals used and subsequent waste generated. the hazardous waste generation rate in a month determines the type of generator and associated regulatory requirements. The three categories of generators are:

Conditionally exempt small-quantity generator

Generates<220 Ib/month Small-quantity generator

Generates 220Ib/month but <2,200Ib/month

Hazardous waste generator Generates 2,200Ib/month

A small-quantity generator may accumulate hazardous waste on site for 180 days or less without a permit, provided that the following conditions specified by the U.S. E.P.A. are met:

- The quantity of hazardous waste accumulated on site never exceeds 13,200 Ib in a calendar month and never exceeds 2.2 Ib of an acutely hazardous waste. The acute wastes are specifically listed in 40 CFR 261.30.
- The material is temporarily stored in accordance with the regulatory requirements for tanks or containers.
- The date on which each period of accumulation begins is clearly marked and visible for inspection on each container.

- The wastes being accumulated on-site are labeled or marked clearly with the words *Hazardous Waste*. This applies to each container and/or tank.
- The facility complies with the requirements to develop a preparedness and prevention plan.
- The facility has a Contingency Plan on-site: At all times there must be at least one employee either on the premises or on call with the responsibility for coordinating all emergency coordinator.
- The generator posts the following information next to the telephone:
  - — the name and telephone number of the emergency coordinator
  - — location of fire extinguishers and spill control material, and, if present, fire alarm
  - — the telephone number of the fire department, unless the facility has a direct alarm
- The generator ensures that the emergency coordinator and all other employees are thoroughly familiar with proper waste handling and emergency procedures. requirements for training are relevant to their responsibilities during normal facility operations and emergencies.

Generator conditions and procedures. During temporary on-site storage of hazardous wastes, a small-quantity generator must adhere to the following conditions and procedures:

- The floor of the storage area must be impervious to leaks and must be free of drains, cracks, or gaps.
- The waste containers must be in good condition, compatible with the waste material, and inspected at least weekly.
- The containers must be kept closed when not in use.
- The containers holding reactive or ignitable wastes must be stored at least 50 ft. inside the property boundary.
- The waste containers must be elevated on pallets to prevent contact with accumulated liquids.

Empty containers. Through standard operating activities, facilities will have empty containers that once held either product or waste. Empty containers consist of steel and plastic drums, drum liners, steel and plastic pails, cardboard drums, and paper bags. Empty containers should be refused and recycled whenever possible. A container or inner liner removed from a container that has previously held any hazardous waste is empty if:

- all possible wastes have been removed using the practices commonly employed to remove materials from that type of container
- no more than 1 in. of residue remains on the

bottom of the container or inner liner; no more than 3% by weight of the total capacity of the container remains in the container or inner liner if the container is < 110 gal in size; or no more than 0.3% by weight of the total capacity of the container remains in the container or inner liner if the container is greater than 110 gal in size.

A container or inner liner removed from a container that has held an acutely hazardous waste is empty if any of the following conditions are met:

- The container or inner liner has been triple rinsed using a solvent capable of removing the commercial chemical product or manufacturing chemical intermediate.
- The container or inner liner has been cleaned by another method that has been proven to achieve equivalent removal.
- The inner liner has been removed.

A container that has held compressed gas in empty if pressure in the container approaches atmospheric pressure.

Labeling. Generators must properly label and prepare shipping papers for each hazardous waste container shipped off-site.

The purpose of a manifest is to keep a record from the time a waste leaves a generator facility to the time it is received at the ultimate disposition facility. Any intermediate storage facility at which waste is stored for more than 10 days or a treatment facility must also be listed on the manifest. The manifest must list an alternate facility if the first choice is unavailable. Each manifest must be retained for three years. Analytical or test results must also be maintained for at least three years. Periods of retention are automatically extended for facilities where enforcement action has occurred. A detailed description of the process and forms used for transporting hazardous was is presented at the end of the RCRA section as part of the discussion of HMTA.

A small-quantity generator is responsible for reporting any manifests of wastes not signed by the disposition facility within 60 days. A legible copy of the manifest with some indication that th generator has not received confirmation of delivery is required to be reported to the regulatory authority. This report mst be sent to the EPA regional administrator for the region in which the generator is located or the state regulatory authority.

Large-quantity generators have 35 days in which to receive the returned manifest before contacting the transporter or disposal facility to determine the status of the hazardous waste. They must submit, within 45 days to the regulatory authority a cover letter explaining their attempts to locate the manifest and a copy of the unreturned manifest.

In general, regulatory requirements become stricter and more burdensome as the quantity of hazardous wastes generated increases and the time they are stored on-site lengthens. some of the strictest requirements are for facilities that meet the regulatory definition as a treatment, long-term storage, or disposal facility.

RCRA characteristics and generators: Summary. The RCRA regulations provide a cradle-to-grave framework for hazardous wastes that covered generators, transporters and treatment, storage, and/or disposal facilities. The first two sections of this chapter discussed characteristics of an RCRA waste and who is considered a "generator." A brief introduction to the transportation rules was presented; however, this area will be covered in greater detail at the conclusion of the RCRA discussion. The next section describes storage of materials.

RCRA storage: Underground Storage tanks

RCRA was substantially amended in 1984. This amendment, known as the Hazardous and Solid Waste Amendments of 1984, revised the RCRA - related statutes to include notification and technical provisions for USTs. The EPA has devoted considerable attention to the problem of USTs; therefore, this section presents a detailed analysis and discussion of the UST problem and regulations.

An UST is a tank that has 10% or more of its volume underground and contains a regulated substance such as:

- petroleum products

- hazardous substances regulated under CERCLA.

History

Since the beginning of this century, it has been the common practice in the United States to store petroleum products and chemicals in buried bare-steel tanks. A 1988 review of the type of tanks in use at gasoline service stations shows that 84% were simple bare steel without leak protection. Initially, both federal and state environmental regulations were more concerned with air and surface water contamination than damage to groundwater. However, by the 1980s, concern began to grow around groundwater protection and the potential impact of leaking USTs. Estimates from the EPA indicate that there are 1.6 million regulated USTs in the United States; in addition, somewhere around 25% of these tanks are believed to be leaking. Thus, the potential for significant groundwater impact is quite high.

Gasoline is the commodity stored in approximately two-thirds of the USTs, with diesel accounting for the other one-third. The underground storage mode had been used for fire safety reasons. USTs containing gasoline and diesel fuel may be found on farms; at service stations; convenience stores; public, private, and military motor pools; airports; marinas; and transportation—related companies.

Causes of leaks

According to EPA studies, the releases from underground storage tanks are typically associated with these problems: (1) piping failure, (2) corrosion, and (3) spills and overfilling. Approximately 80% of the underground releases at gasoline service stations involve improperly installed piping systems. Two types of piping systems are commonly in use. In type 1, a pressure system operates with pressure in the tanks to push the product through the piping and dispensing unit. his type of pressure system is more prone to releases during pumping, because the tanks' contents will continue to be pushed out of any break(s) in the piping. Type 2 piping configuration is a suction system. This system is less likely to experience large volume piping supplies because once a leak occurs, the vacuum is lost and the product flows back to the tank.

Corrosion of the tank is another common cause of underground storage tank leakage. Hundreds of thousands of tanks installed in the United States were fabricated of bare steel without adequate leak protection. Many of these tanks have corroded and are leaking.

The third problem, spills and overfills, is the most common cause of releases to the environment from underground storage tanks. Typically, these spills and overfills are small in volume, i.e., less than 20 gal, and are infrequently reported. Spills often take place during deliveries, when improper hose drainage occurs. Overfills can be attributed in many cases to carelessness during tank-filling operations.

Materials stored

Both the retail and nonretail sections of business and commerce use USTs for storage of motor fuels, used oil, and hazardous chemicals. Non-retail motor fuel is approximately 38% and includes agriculture, petroleum wholesalers, commercial transportation, and governmental motor pools.

Regulations for USTs

Until 1984, a limited number of federal regulations addressed UST issues. Because underground tanks containing a petroleum product with a capacity in excess of 42,000 gal could be a direct source of pollution in navigable waters, tank owners/operators have been required, under the Federal Water Pollution Control Act Amendments of 1972 to prepare and implement when necessary a spill prevention control and countermeasure plan (SPCC), Part of the SPCC plan required corrosion protection and pressure testing of underground storage tanks. However, the CWA impacted few underground tanks, because USTs are generally a threat to groundwater rather than surface water. Furthermore, the RCRA regulations of 1976 had jurisdiction only for tanks that contained hazardous wastes. Thus, there was a regulatory gap; RCRA did not address USTs that contained hazardous products or petroleum.

Further complicating this regulatory commission was specific CERCLA exemption for petroleum tank leaks. Although CERCLA is specifically directed toward hazardous substance leaks, USTs were to covered. Petroleum tank leaks account for the bulk of reported UST leaks.

To close this obvious regulatory gap, the Hazardous and Solid Waste Amendments to RCRA were signed into law in 1984. The USTs were brought into the mainstream of regulations via Title VI, Subtitle I of HSWA. The Subtitle I key provisions include: notification requirements, monitoring and reporting standards, tank standards, financial responsibility, corrective actin, compliance monitoring and enforcement, and state programs approval. HSWA mandated that the EPA establish a full-scale program for UST regulations that would protect hun ın health and the environment. The EPA's Office of Underground Storage Tanks developed regulations for technical tank standards, including leak-detection methods and tank construction materials. These standards are set forth in the September 1988 EPA brochure called "Musts for USTs." In October 1988, EPA produced financial responsibility regulations that stipulated the minimum amounts of insurance needed by owners and/or operators to assure their ability to implement corrective action in the even of a leaking UST.

SARA/UST trust fund

The HSWA did not address how to deal with leaking tanks when th owners could not be found or when they were unable or unwilling to take the appropriate corrective action to deal with leaders. Congress again reacted to public concern by generating the Superfund Amendments and Reauthorization Act in 1986.

Section 205 of SARA revised RCRA Subtitle I so

that federal money became available in order to remediate UST petroleum leaks and spills. A $500 million Leaking Underground Storage Tank Trust Fund was established. The monies were to be generated by a five-year tax on all gasoline sales.

Additionally, the Trust Fund has been made available to the states to increase response time to LUSTs. cooperative agreements have been signed between the EPA and those states that were interested in accessing the Trust Fund for cleanup purposes. The Trust Fund was not intended for most LUSTs, because the state governments normally direct the responsible party to handle the cleanup. The SARA amendments give the states the authority to direct the responsible party to:

- test suspected tanks for leaks
- excavate to determine the degree of contamination
- remove the contaminants from water and/or soil
- determine individuals who were exposed to the contamination
- make safe drinking water available to persons who have had their source of water contaminated by the leak
- if conditions dictate, relocate residents who have been adversely affected by the spill or leak.

Congress was aware that cleanups and compensation operations could be costly.

Therefore, a minimum insurance coverage of $1 million for each occurrence at locations that refine, produce, and/or market petroleum was established. Thus, the EPA or a state use the Trust Fund only when (1) cleanup cost exceeds the minimum insurance required and additional funds are needed to ensure a successful job, (2) a solvent owner/operator can't be located, or (3) the owner/ operator refuses to abide by a cleanup order.

EPA office of underground storage tanks

In mid-1985, the Office of Underground Storage Tanks (OUST) was established under the auspices of the Office of Solid Waste and Emergency Response (OSWER). The EPA organization was composed of a headquarters unit and 10 regional offices located around the country. With the creation of OUST, a manager and staff were sited at each of the regional offices.

The EPA recognized that the OUST program would require different management techniques than other EPA regulatory programs. The large number of leaking tanks throughout the United States outstripped EPA's ability to successfully deal with the issue. This led EPA to develop a franchise model for the state. This model encourages flexibility and the use of innovative approaches in solving problems to the local level. Once a state or local regulatory agency sings a franchise agreement with EPA, it functions independently. From that point on, the EPA serves as a clearinghouse for ideas and relays information and data to the franchised state or local agency. This enables the authorized agency to develop viable UST programs and operate with one set of regulations. Each franchisee must meet, as a minimum, the federal requirements in these areas:

- new UST system design construction, installation, and notification.
- upgradng of existing UST systems
- general operating requirements
- release detection
- release reporting, investigation, and confirmation
- corrective action
- out-of-service or closed UST systems
- financial responsibility.

In 1993, 12 states were operating under the franchise provisions, with certain other states functioning with a memorandum of understanding.

New installation requirements

A new installation is deemed to be an UST system that has been installed after December 1988. The criteria for new installations are complex and cover five areas: (1) design and installation, (2) corrosion protection, (3) leak detection, (4) corrective measures, and (5) closure procedures and record keeping. New chemical USTs and pre-1980 system requirements and upgrades will also be covered at the end of this discussion.

Design and installation. The design and installation requirements are listed here, along with best management practices to prevent leaks.

- *Proper installation*—the owner/operator is obliged to follow industry practices and standards. A good reference is the booklet entitled "Installation of Underground Petroleum Storage Systems" by the American Petroleum Institute. A second valuable reference is the EPA's video "Doing It Right."

  Improper installation is a significant cause of failure for both Fiberglas and steel tanks, particularly for the piping systems. Qualified installers who follow the industry codes are the key to successful installations. During the installation process, attention must be focused on developing good plans, placement of the tank and related equipment, the excavation, depth of burial, assembly of all components, tank anchoring, backfill, and final grading and surfacing.

- *Notification*—At the time of installation, it is required that the owner/operator inform the state agency on the appropriate notification form that the new UST is being installed. The services of a qualified installer who certifies that the job was done correctly are required.

- *Spill and overfills protection*—The majority of spills and overfills results from operator error. It is important for the owner/operator to follow correct tank filling practices; in addition, required mechanical devices must be on line. Specifically:

- Step 1 is to determine whether the capacity of the receiving tank exceeds the volume of material that is being transferred to it.
- Step 2 is to ensure that the entire transfer operation is constantly watched.
- Step 3 is to install equipment that prevents both spills and overfills. this is mandatory for new USTs. Overfill devices include automatic flow shutoffs, flow resistors, and full tank alarms that actuate when a tank in nearing capacity during the filling process. Spill prevention devices are items such as catch basins and hose couplings rigged with a dry disconnect. Existing tanks are required to have spill and overfill devices by December 1998.

Corrosion protection. When unprotected steel is buried in the earth, it is exposed to a natural electrochemical environment and/or to artificially generated direct electrical currents in the burial area. When these electrical conditions are combined with moisture, a situation is produced that can corrode steel. Technology to combat this corrosive process has existed for years. Many UST systems have been well protected from the time of installation. However, in numerous cases, protective measures were not undertaken and bare, unprotected steel USTs were buried. These unprotected tanks are subject to corrosion, pitting, and leakage. Corrosion prevention is required in the EPA regulations, 40 CFR Part 280, for both new and existing tanks. This requirement became effective in December 1988. Another source of potential corrosive leakage is piping.

There are four options for new USTs and piping:

- Use steel tanks that are coated with a protective layer of a corrosion-resistant material and that also ave cathodic protection the Cathodic protection can be either in the form of sacrificial anode attached to the tank and piping or by introducing a direct current into the ground around the UST system via anodes that are not attached to the system.
- Employ the use of fiberglass tanks. when fiberglass is used, it is vital to ensure that the fiberglass is compatible with the stored material. Also, proper bedding of the tank and backfilling of the excavation is crucial in order to avoid damage.
- Use composite tanks constructed with a thick layer of fiberglass bonded to the exterior of a steel tank. Any damage to the fiberglass on a composite tank will negate its corrosion resistance; therefore, careful handling, inspection, and installation, are required. Cathodic protection on composite tanks is not required by the federal regulations; however, certain states do require cathodic protection. Therefore, tank installers must check state and/or local regulations prior to installation.
- Use systems that are "no less protective of human health and the environment" than the

first three approaches. This option encourages new technology. One technique employed in this category is to install steel tanks and piping with nonmetallic jackets.

Tank leak detection. The criteria for new or upgraded petroleum USTs leak detection are as follows;

- The methods chosen must be accurate enough to detect leakage in any part of the tank and piping that contains petroleum on a regular basis.
- The manufacturer's direction must be adhered to relative to the installation, calibration, maintenance, and operation of the equipment.
- Federal regulations sections 280.43 and 280.44 of title 40 list the performance criteria for the leak-detection equipment.
- One approach is to drill *monitoring wells* in the vicinity of the UST. These wells are checked regularly to determine whether any product has leaked and is accumulating on or in the water table. The detection within the wells can be either manual or automatic. Another method is to monitor for *vapours* in the soil adjacement to an UST. This method is suitable only where porous backfill materials has been used around the tank.

Processes that automatically evaluate the *product volume* and compare it with the inventory figures are an acceptable means of detecting leaks. *Interstitial monitoring* is another technique employed to detect leaks. Instruments monitor the space between the UST and a double wall, partial barrier, or tank liner. With this approach it is possible to detect tank leaks before the contamination has spread to soil and/or groundwater.

Piping leak detection. As previously mentioned piping systems can either be the pressure or suction type. For a pressure piping system, the owner/operator must use automatic line leak detection. Also, an annual line tightness test or monthly leak-detection monitoring must be employed.

For a suction piping system, leak detection is not required if (1) the buried piping is installed with a downgrade slope to the tank so that the product will automatically run back to the tank if the suction is lost, and (2) the system is designed with only one check valve that is located immediately beneath the suction pump. If a suction piping system does not meet these criteria, the owner/operator must conduct either a line tightness test every three years or monthly leak-direction procedure.

Corrective measures. If there is reason to believe that an UST system is leaking, prompt action is necessary. If leakage is confirmed, an action plan with aopropriate corrective measures is required to be implemented as follows.

1. Take immediate action in order to stop the leak spill and contain the material.

2. Make certain that the incident will not threaten human life or health by way of explosive vapors or drinking water contamination.
3. Report the incident to the regulatory agency within 24 hour unless it involves less than 25 gallons of petroleum and the spill was promptly contained and cleaned up.
4. Assess the full extent of the leaked material and implement the recovery of spilled material.
5. Report the cleanup progress to the regulatory agency no later than 20 days after the incident is confirmed.
6. Assess within 45 days existing or potential damage to the environment and report to the appropriate regulatory personnel. If groundwater is contaminated, a detailed report of the cleanup action plan must be submitted to the agency.

On a long-term basis, the information transmitted to the regulators could result in an agency-mandated corrective action plan. Repairing of USTs is a acceptable if the standard industry codes for repair work are addressed. Within 30 days of a repair, the integrity of the tank must be demonstrated by one of the following procedures:

- Internally inspecting the tank or conducting a tightness test per industry code.
- Applying any of the monthly leak test

procedures with the exception of the inventory control/tank tightness test method.

- Employing other techniques approved by the regulatory authority. Repaired USTs that are equipped with cathodic protection must be checked to prove that the cathodic system is correctly functioning. Repair records must be maintained for the duration of time that the UST is kept in service.
- Leaking piping must be replaced, not repaired. Metallic pipe joints that have merely loosened may be tightened. If national codes of practice or the manufacture's procedures are followed, fiberglass-reinforced plastic piping may be repaired. As in the case of repaired tanks, a test is required within 30 days; however, internal inspections are obviously not appropriate for piping systems.

When considering whether to repair and/or upgrade existing UST systems, the owner/operator may want to employ the services of a corrosion engineer who specializes in this type of work.

Closure procedures and recordkeeping. USTs may be closed on either a temporary or a permanent basis. Tanks that lack corrosion protection and that stay closed in excess of 12 months and tanks that have been selected for closure must adhere to those permanent closure requirements.

- The regulators must be given a 30-day advance closure notice.
- The surrounding area must be checked for

leakage. If leakage exists, then the procedures previously discussed are necessary.

- The tank must be emptied, cleaned of any sludge, vapors, and/or liquids. This process can be quite hazardous. A tank that is being decommissioned may present a flammable/ explosive condition or may contain toxic residuals.

These jobs should only be performed by personnel who have been properly trained, with the correct equipment and personal protective gear, and who follow all pertinent health and safety practices.

Once the tank is drained and cleaned per the accepted practices, it may be left in the ground or removed. If it remains in the ground, it must be filled with an inert solid material such as sand.

Permanent closure requirements do not apply to an UST if any one of these items is met.

- When the UST in question meets the criteria for a new or upgraded unit, it can be placed in temporarily closed status for as long as it continues to fulfill the temporarily closed requirements.
- USTs that are not protected from corrosion can be granted an extension of the 12-month temporary closure limit by the regulatory authority that has jurisdiction.
- The contents of a tank can be changed to unregulated material. However, the owner/

operator must first notify the regulators, empty and clean the tank, survey the surrounding environment for contamination, and perform the appropriate cleanup measures where indicated.

Temporary closure. Temporary closure pertains to tanks that are not used for 3 to 12 months. USTs with leak detection and corrosion prevention in place must be maintained with these systems on-line. In the event of a leak, the response will be in the normal manner. If the tank is empty, there is not a requirement to operate the leak-detection system. While the UST is temporarily closed, all lines, except the vent, must be capped.

Reporting. When an UST is installed, the state in which it is located must be informed by submitting a notification form. All existing USTs should already have been reported by this process.

Releases of both a suspect and confirmed nature must be reported. In the case of confirmed releases that result in damage, the follow-up action plan also must be submitted. Thirty days prior to the permanent closure of an UST, the regulatory personnel must be notified.

Record keeping. The records at a site cover four major sectors. (1) the functioning and maintenances of the leak-detection systems (includes information such as performance specification data provided by manufacturer, the previous year's monitoring results and the most current tightness test, and recent calibration and maintenance records) (2) the availability of thereports from the professional who performed the last two corrosion system inspections; (3) the documents that show that upgrades and repairs were properly executed; and (4) the records of the site assessments for three years after any permanent closure.

New chemical USTs/existing USTs

Hundreds of chemicals are listed as hazardous in the comprehensive environmental response compensation and liability act of 1980. The UST regulations apply to storage of all chemical products and substances. Hazardous wastes regulated under subtitle C of RCRA are not regulated under the UST program.

New chemical USTs. Systems installed after December 1988 must adhere to the same requirements as apply to new petroleum USTs. These requirements include proper design and installation, corrosion prevention, spill and overflow protection, corrective measures, record-keeping, and closure procedures. In addition, chemical USTs are required to be installed with secondary containment and interstitial monitoring. Secondary containment can be achieved by installing the tank or piping inside a second tank and pipe creating a double-walled system. Another alternative is to place a system inside a concrete vault or third, line the excavation with an impermeable membrane when the tank system is installed. Interstitial monitoring is achieved in the previously described fashion, i.e., monitor the space between the walls.

Existing petroleum UST requirements. Systems that were installed prior to December 1988 are considered to be "existing" USTs. Tank-filling procedures that eliminate spills and overfills were required to be in effect by 1933. By December 1998, spill and overfill prevention devices, such as catch basins and overfill alarms, must be in place. Also by December 1988, existing steel tanks and piping are required to have corrosion protection.

Corrosion protection can be achieved by a corrosion-resistant coating and cathodic protection or by other suitable methods that the regulatory authority approves. The EPA phased in the leak-detection requirement over a five-year period based on the age of the tank. However, the phase-in period ended in December 1993. Compliance with the leak-detection provision is achieved from one of these three options.

- Monthly monitoring of liquids on the groundwater, vapors in the soil, interstitial, or automatic tank gauging.
- Tanks that have a lining, corrosion protection, or spills- and overflow-prevention devices can use monthly inventory control in conjunction with tightness testing on 5-year intervals. This procedure is acceptable for only 10 years after the tank has been lined or rigged with corrosion protection or until December 1998. whichever date is later. Monthly monitoring must be used after 10 years. Monthly inventory control in conjunction with annual tank tightness tests are presently acceptable

for existing USTs without corrosion control, internal linings, and spills-and overflow-prevention devices. However, this approach is valid only until December 1998. By then, all USTs must have corrosion protection or be lined and outfitted with spills-and overflow-prevention devices. Additionally, the previously discussed leak-detection methods must be used.

Existing pipe leak detection. The choices for pipe leak detection depend on the type of piping system. As of December 1990, existing pressure systems must adhere to the same detection criteria established for new systems. Existing suction systems must follow the same phase-in schedule that has been established for existing tanks. As of December 1993, the existing suction piping systems must meet the leak-detection criteria previously listed for new installations.

RCRA storage: aboveground storage tanks

The only RCRA regulations requiring proper containment of an oily substances are EPA's title 40, part 279 regulations on the subject of waste oil. A greater of waste oil has the responsibility under this part to properly store and oversee final disposition of waste oils. No specific storage or tank containment requirements exist for noncommercial waste oil businesses, but improper disposal is prohibited.

Other requirements, such as the clean water act regulations, given potentially spilled petroleum substances. The EPA's oil pollution prevention regulations have been in effect since 1973. The oil pollution act of 1980 amended these regulations to address nontransportation-related facilities. A spill prevention control and countermeasure plan is required of anyone who stores petroleum substances that could be released into U.S. waters.

Many states require plans for both petroleum substances and hazardous substances when there is a potential of such substances leaking into state waters. Spill response plans related to SPCCs are discussed in the sections of this chapter that address CERCLA. This section is directed toward control strategies that can be applicable to aboveground oil storage facilities;

- *Coverage*. Facilities that drill, produce, gather, store, process, refine, transfer, and/or consume oil products are covered by the SPCC regulations if; (1) the operation is not transportation related; (2) a single aboveground container has a capacity in excess of 660 gal (2,500 l), the aggregate aboveground storage capacity exceeds 1,320 gal (5,0001), or the total underground storage exceeds 42,000 gal (159,001); (3) because of the location of the operation, it is probable for an oil spill to reach U.S. waters or adjoining shorelines. The owners/operators of covered facilities must prepare and maintain on site an SPCC plan that has been certified by a registered professional engineer. The plan must be reviewed every three years.
- *Containment*. Containment systems can be

effective in controlling spilled materials. Routing of spilled materials to structures such as sumps, dikes, curbed holding areas, and diversion ponds are effective ways to prevent potential pollutant sources from being released to surface waters. Materials collected in these structures can then be treated and disposed of appropriately. Contingency plans are reactive in nature but necessary when positive containment is impractical because of space limitations.

- *Drainage.* Diked storage areas must be equipped with valves or other equipment in order to prevent oil leaks from escaping via drainage systems. General plant drainage systems from areas that are not diked should be designed to retain oil in catch basins or to route it back to the facility foe refuse or recycling.
- *Bulk tanks.* Oil storage tanks must be designed and built to handle the anticipated storage material. Compatibility of materials, pressure, and temperature must be considered in such designs. Secondary containment that will hold the contents of the largest tank plus extra capacity for rainwater, etc. is required by regulation.
- *Loading and unloading facilities.* Railway tank car and tank truck loading/unloading facilities must adhere to the U.S. Department of transportation regulations. Each loading and unloading rack should be built with a

containment system that will accommodate the capacity of the single largest compartment in any of the tank cars or trucks that service the facility.

- *Security*. Operations that handle oil and covered under an SPCC plan should be equipped with fences and lockable gates. All gates should be locked or posted with guards if the plant is not functioning.
- *Barrelled storage*. Areas where materials are stored in barrels or drums should be sited so as to protect the drums from weather and physical damage. Containment is another important criteria. The entire facility is curbed and sloped to a recovery sump that has a pump. The facility presents an environmentally sound means of dealing with potential spills from barrelled materials.

Disposal: land disposal requirements/siting storage facilities

As previously discussed, the rules governing the storage of hazardous wastes or potentially tightened. Similarly, the ability to use land disposal for hazardous wastes has also been substantially restricted. Typically, land disposal is defined to include placement of waste materials in a:

- concrete vault
- injection well
- landfill

- surface impoundment
- waste pile

The federal government has banned land disposal for certain hazardous wastes that can migrate through soil and pollute groundwater. Hazardous wastes covered by the land ban include liquid metals, free cyanides, dioxin-containing wastes, and discarded chemical products like xylene, formic acid, and methyl alcohol. The ban also prohibits land disposal of diesel fuel, hydrochloric acid, and used solvents without proper treatment or certification of limited recycling options.

The land ban became effective for most spend solvent in November 1986.

Land disposal is restricted unless.

- the wastes meet federal treatment standards
- a quantity of less than 220 lb is generated per month [less than 2,25 lb of acutely hazardous waste]
- the generator obtains a variance from the EPA
- the waste involved soil or debts from a response action under superfund or corrective action under the RCRA.

Facilities that produce hazardous waste streams clearly have a difficult storage problem. The obvious thrust of current regulations and land ban storage requirements is to emphasize waste minimization and treatment options. Unfortunately, a variety of processes and daily activities will continues to produce hazardous waste streams requiring adequate treatment, storage, and disposal alternatives. The siting of TSD facilities is controversial and highly influenced by the local political climate.

Siting of hazardous waste facilities

Several general locational criteria exist when sites for hazardous waste treatment, storage, and disposal facilities are selected. In selecting a location, the first concern should be to protect humans and the environment from the adverse effects of toxic or hazardous waste exposure. The area selected for the facility should be a remote area and/or one with a low population density.

The advantages to selecting areas of low population density include reduced land use potential and minimal effect in the event of a release. One disadvantages of selecting areas of low population density is the distance to urban industrial operation where most wastes are generated. the increased distance from generation to TSDs inevitably increases the chances for a transportation accident.

The site considerations should also include areas where the hydrogeology minimizes possible migration and where the slope of the site itself restricts possible migration of leachate or other waste residues. Public health and welfare, water quality standards, and land use plans should all be evaluated. The site should not be close to wetlands, streams, rivers, lakes, ponds, or reservoirs. The site should be at a minimum 0.25

mi from any well used to supply water and should not impact any well in a shallow aquifer. A new TSD facility in the United States cannot be within 200 ft of a fault in Holocene time, i.e., the most recent geologic period. Also, the facility can not be built within 100-year flood plains unless the waste can be removed safely before a flood.

Specifications for container storage of hazardous waste tanks include soil conductivity. The soil must not corrode the tank to any extent that may potentially impact human health and welfare. With surface impoundments, a liner must be placed on a surface that will not uplift, compress, or settle. Double-lined surface impoundments may be exempt from groundwater monitoring if the bottom is above the seasonal high-water table. Landfills should be above the groundwater table, and land treatment units should be 3.28 ft above the seasonal high water table.

Complete environmental monitoring procedures are required to be documented in a closure plan to decontaminate and/or decommission facility equipment, buildings, and hazardous wastes. Documentation is required for all soil, groundwater, and surface water sampling results, including effluent quality monitoring conducted at the site during the history of operations. A detailed description of the location, collection, chain of custody, methodology, analysis, laboratory, quality assurance/control procedures, and other applicable records should be retained and available.

Criteria levels and rankings

The following levels of criteria and subsequent ranking pertain to selecting hazardous waste sites.

Level-1 criteria. Level-1 criteria are technically defensible criteria that identify and eliminate clearly unacceptable areas and in some instances that identify areas with higher potential for containing suitable sites, including:

- costal flood hazard areas
- costal wetland
- debase or basalt bedrock areas
- anthracite mining
- public water supply watersheds
- aquifer/well yield
- critical recharges areas
- aquicludes
- seismic risk zones
- natural areas of designated county, state, regional, or national significance.

Level-2 criteria. Criteria at the second level include land use, zoning, and infrastructure that identify candidate sites suitable for detailed screening, including:

- lands designed for industrial use
- sites of existing facilities
- dedicated lands in public trust
- arterial highways.

Level-3 criteria. level-3 criteria are technically based and detailed site-specific criteria that exclude outright a site from further consideration and indicate general suitability in terms of "negative," "neutral," and "positive" ratings, including;

- riverine flood hazard areas
- stream proximity and use
- stream flow and quality
- aquifer use
- groundwater flow systems
- groundwater quality
- geologic faults
- unconsolidated deposits
- bedrock
- of mineral development
- slope
- prime agricultural land
- soil permeability, soil pH
- solid cation exchanges capacity
- freshwater wetlands
- critical habitat for rare and endangered species
- nearshore commercial shellfish resources
- historic places

- air quality designation
- structures along transportation corridor
- transportation restrictions
- population density in vicinity of facility
- proximity to incompatible facilities/structures
- site ownership.

Ranking system. the following suggested procedure can be used for preliminary site selection:

1. Level-3 criteria ratings are determined for each factor at each site.
2. The number of "negative" and "positive" ratings are totaled for each site.
3. The sites are ranked in two lists, one list for the number of "negative" ratings and the other for the number of "positive" ratings.
4. The quartile having the fewest "negative" ratings and the most "positive" ratings is identified.
5. The identified sites from each list are combined, in no particular order, in a new list.

Final site selection. For the final list of suitable sites, fields and laboratory investigations are conducted to verify data and to get more detail, public hearings are held to consider political and social concerns.

RCRA transportation: moving hazardous materials

The transportation of hazardous materials impacts virtually all aspects of the business community.

When the movement is performed safely and efficiently, actitivites such as a tank truck distributing motor fuel, a vacuum truck carrying spent solvents, a bulk carrier bringing crude oil from a distant land, or an air parcel service delivering needed chemicals just in time to prevent a shutdown of a production line are routine.

Unfortunately, unsafe acts associated with the transportation of hazardous materials can cause incidents such as oil spills from tanker accidents, chemicals releases and fires from train derailments, or aircraft making forced landings because of a spill of improperly packaged chemicals. Fortunately, the transportation industry and regulatory bodies are working together to create standards that, when properly implemented, will prevent such incidents from occurring.

The first legislation regulating the transportation of hazardous materials-the United States rail transportation safety act of 1906-was enacted to help eliminate accidents caused by hazardous materials transported by rail. After a number of rail incidents involving explosives, the government decided that more extensive legislation was necessary.

As other modes of transport evolved, so did the hazardous material transport regulations, eventually expanding to include vessel, highway, and finally air regulations. These regulations were codified under title 49 of the code of federal regulations, and were the model for most other regulations worldwide. However, the United States regulations have gradually grown apart from those recognized internationally. In an effort to more closely align 49 CFR with the rest of the world's regulations, commonly known as HM-181, recent changes have been made to update 49 CFR. These standards are being phased in gradually and will be completely implemented by the year 2000.

The standards of 49 CFR are administered by the U.S. Department of transportation. Within the DOT is the research and special programs administration. RSPA is responsible for developing a national regulatory program to protect against the risks to life and property inherent in the transportation of hazardous material by all modes. Embodied in this regulatory program is the responsibility for the promulgation of hazardous materials regulations that are codified at subchapter C of 49 CFR. Heavy reliance is placed on participation of the four modal administrations in the regulatory process.

In a 1985 reorganization of RSPA, the office of Hazardous materials transportation assumed the responsibility for regulating hazardous materials under the hazardous materials transportation act. The regulations address classification, packaging, handling, incident reporting, and hazard communication of hazardous materials. These regulations are continually reviewed to address safety concerns and to eliminate obsolete or unnecessary requirements.

Along with regulatory development, enforcement actions, and training, OHMT also publishers the *Emergency response guidebook*, which provides guidance for initial actions to be taken by emergency responders to hazardous materials incidents. The *Guidebook* addresses all hazardous materials regulated by the DOT, along with suggested initial response actions in the event of an incident involving regulated hazardous materials. The guidebook is updated periodically to accommodate new products and changes in technology. It is available to first responders, police, fire, and other emergency response personnel. OHMT's goal is to have the guidebook in every emergency response vehicle nationwide. To date, more than 2.5 million copies have been distributed, without charge, to the emergency response community.

A related set of transportation regulations is administered by the U.S. EPA for hazardous wastes. These standards, found in 40 CFR 263, address the manifesting, transporting, and tracking of shipments of hazardous waste. The DOT hazardous materials standards for classifying, packaging, and labeling are incorporated into the EPA regulations by reference. The hazardous waste transportation standards are part of the overall EPA cradle-to-grave hazardous waste management philosophy and are in place largely to establish accountability and responsibility for the waste as it is moved from the generator to a treatment, storage, disposal, or final disposition facility.

Significant penalties are associated with breaks in the "chain of custody" as it relates to the proper handling and disposal of hazardous waste. The following discussion presents a more detailed description of the labeling and manifesting requirements for off-site shipments of hazardous wastes.

Procedure for labeling, manifesting, and tracking hazardous wastes

Shipment for off-site disposal requires the completion of a hazardous waste label and manifest. Instructions for their completion are described here.

Hazardous waste label. The yellow hazardous waste label shown earlier must be completed for all containers being shipped and must be prominently displayed on the container. The following information is required on the label.

- name of generator
- address
- phone
- EPA ID number
- manifest document number
- accumulation start date
- EPA waste number
- proper DOT shipping name
- UN or NA number.

The accumulation start date should be completed at the time waste is first collected in the drum in the accumulation area. The generator information should be completed on the label. The remaining information-proper DOT shipping name, UN or NA number, and EPA waste number-should also be complete and checked for accuracy by the responsible supervisor/manager.

The manifest document number is from the manifest under which the container will be shipped. A manifest document number appears on the top line of the manifest. It is a number the own/operator has assigned to the document foe tracking purposes. This connects the container with a particular shipment of waste.

Hazardous waste manifest. Hazardous waste may not be moved outside the immediate vicinity of the source facility without an EPA-approved manifest. The manifest is basically a special shipping paper that contains certain important information about the waste.

- where it came from (the "generator" of the waste)
- where it is going (TSD facility)
- who is taking it from the generator to the TSD facility (the "transporter")
- what the waste is
- how much waste is included in the shipment
- what kind of and how many containers are in the shipment
- what kind of hazard the waste can cause.

In addition, personnel representing the generator, the transporter, and the TSD facility must sign special statements on the manifest. These statements say that personnel have examined the drums of waste and found the information to agree with the manifest. This information verifies that the containers are proper for the waste being shipped, the counts or weights match those on the manifest, and the wastes in the containers are the wastes listed on the manifest.

It is important to remember the manifest is the special shipping paper, and that to *manifest* means to transport a shipment with an accompanying special shipping paper, or manifest.

However, in states that issue their own manifest forms, those forms must be used for wastes being shipped intrastate as well as interstate. Typically, the form has an original with five carbon copies.

Usually, the supervisor/manger or environmental coordinator prepares the manifest for each off-site shipment. The supervisor/manger is responsible for ensuring that the waste indicated on the manifest is the waste being provided to the transporter. The manifest must then he dated and signed. The transporter also signs the manifest and provides one copy of the multicopy form to the shipper's representatives. This manifest must be retained by the owner/operator of the generating waste facility.

A manifest must be prepared if a hazardous

waste is going to be shipped off-site. If an owner/ operator is not shipping the waste off-site, but for example., moving it from one are of the building to another, a manifest is not required.

Tracking the manifest. The operator of the transportation vehicle will take all copies of the manifest except the shipper's copy, which the owner/operator retains. The shipper's copy must be kept in an appropriate file and maintained buy the originator's facility. Once the disposal facility receives the shipment and signs the manifest, the original copy will be returned to the owner/ operator. It must be retained along with the shipper's copy in an appropriate file.

The original plus the shipper's copy are considered a *matched pair*. It is an assurance that the waste has been documented from its generation through its transportation to its disposal. If an original is not returned from a disposal facility within 30 days of shipment, the owner/operator must be notified.

Pretransportation procedures. The owner/ operator schedules shipments. When the transporter calls to confirm a shipment, the owner/operator must be certain that;

- All containers in the shipment are DOT-specification containers and are in good shape.
- The containers have been properly marked and labeled (the hazardous wastes warning sticker has been completely filled out) or confirm who will be responsible for providing completed labels.

- The manifest has been filled out or a designated person will complete the information required by the manifest.

Transfer of shipment to transporter. When the transporter arrives to pick up the shipment of hazardous wastes, a supervisor/manger or EC of the facility should be present. The supervisor/manger or EC is responsible for the proper transfer of the waste to the transporter. A manifest must be completed and signed as described in this section. The operator must be provided with a copy of the signed manifests and the generator's copy must be retained by the owner/operator in the facility files for three years. If the transportation vehicle is in disrepair, not properly placarded, or the "operator" does not appear to be in proper condition, the supervisor/manger or EC should refuse to release the waste to the transporter.

Waste tracking. Generators are required to maintain records of hazardous waste activities for three years. The files to be retained facility that received the waste, a copy of each biennial report and exception report, inspection logs, and records of any rest results, waste analyses, or other hazardous waste determination. All records should be kept for as long as the operator is in business, although the requirement is three years.

The next section moves from the specific U.S. transportation rules to a broader international perspective on hazardous materials transportation.

International transportation

By their very nature, air and water transportation of hazardous materials seem to be more conducive to internationally recognized regulations than are rail or highway transport. Currently, no centralized international organization regulates the transportation of hazardous materials by either rail or highway. the increasing cooperation within the European Union may help standardize ground transport within europe, but it appears that the regulations in other parts of the world will continue to be left to individual governments. However, the international community has taken steps to establish standards for air and water transportation of hazardous materials.

During the 1950s air transport became more common, and international. Air transport Association an industry organization of the world's airlines, concluded it was virtually impossible for the shipping public to comply with each government's different regulations in international shipping. As a result, in 1959 IATA developed the first set of shipping regulations known as the IATA Dangerous Goods Regulations. These regulations are recognized worldwide for the air transport of hazardous materials. Using the input of scientists, chemists, shippers, airline industry experts, and eventually packaging engineers, IATA developed regulations and packaging standards according to a material's properties and it possible hazardous reactions during air transport. IATA's jurisdiction as a regulatory entity was assumed by the International civil Aviation Organization in

1983. Although no longer considered the governing body for air transport, IATA has grown to include more than 200 of the world's airlines and continues to have a tremendous influence on the air regulations. Published annually, the IATA dangerous Goods Regulations mirror the ICAO Technical Instructions and continue to be the regulations used by the airline industry and shippers alike, due to their straightforward, easy-to-understand format.

Under the jurisdiction of the united Nations, the ICAO is an organization of government representatives from around the world. In 1983, the ICAO became involved in the rules for the air transport of hazardous materials and began publishing what became the internationally recognized regulations for the air transport of hazardous materials.

The "ICAO technical Instructions for the Transport of Dangerous Goods by air" are recognized by most countries and usually may be used in place of the individual country's regulations. for example, DOT standards permit air carriers to follow either DOT or ICAO representatives meet twice a year, issuing revised ICAO technical Instructions each time.

The International Maritime Organization is the vessel transport equivalent of ICAO. A worldwide organization of government representatives, the IMO began developing the international regulations for hazardous materials transportation by water in 1983. As a "sister" organization to ICAO, the IMO is also under the jurisdiction of the United Nations.

Although not as well-organized or as influential as ICAO, the IMO is the recognized governing body for the vessel transport throughout the world. The IMO publishes the International Maritime Dangerous Goods Regulations, which has a classification and numbering system for hazardous materials similar to that found in the ICAO criteria.

Hazardous materials transport regulations

Most countries still have their own regulations for domestic transport, but the advent of the IATA dangerous Goods Regulations in 1959 helped to significantly and permanently change the shipping requirements for all types of transport. the IATA regulations allowed one common set of rules to be used by shippers worldwide. After these rules proved to provide a workable solution to a difficult problem, other organizations began to follow suit, including the IMO/LMDG regulations for hazardous materials transported by vessel-which have become closely aligned with ICAO/LATA. Although regulations for highway and rail transport are still generally determined by each country, most countries have-or are beginning to-align their regulations with the ICAO and IMO requirements.

Revisions to DOT regulations

As noted previously, U.S. DOT regulations are changing and will be in fairly close alignment with other major organizations by the year 2000.

This discussion describes the major revisions to these standards.

HM-181. Passed by congress in 1990, the hazardous materials transportation uniform safety act is an amendment that establishes a phased updating of 49 CFR over a period of time. When these updates are completed in 2000,49 CFR will be in fairly close alignment with the international regulation. HM-181 will (1) introduce a hazard class number system to 49 CFR, (2) recognize United Nations packaging as the only acceptable type of packaging to be used, and (3) affect some other requirements as well.

Of particular interest to the environmental remediation industry are the HM-181 requirements for the packaging and shipping of potentially contaminated samples to analytical laboratories. A new environmentally hazardous substance category has been created that encompasses most of these samples, but the more highly hazardous types of samples may fall into more respective categories. Restrictions on hazardous wastes require such stringnent precautions that packaging costs for samples for air shipment can be prohibitive.

HM-126. Companion legislation that was also passed by congress in 1991, hazardous materials bill 126 contains two very significant provisions.

- Subpart C requires that an emergency response telephone number be shown on the documentation for any shipment; this number must be monitored 24 hours a day by a person who is knowledgeable of the risks associated with the shipped material, and the proper emergency response procedures. This telephone number may not be for an answering machine or paging device. In addition, subpart C requires that a copy of emergency response procedures by provided with the shipment.

- Subpart F requires that "Hazmat Employers" provide training to and test their "Hazmat Employees" regarding safe loading, unloading, handling, storing, and transporting of hazardous materials and mergencuy preparedness foe responding to accidents or incidents involving the transportation of hazardous materials. The training categories include general awareness/familiarization, which provides instruction in basic HM-181 and hazard comunication requirements; Function-specific, in which the Hazmat Employee leanrs package and shipping techniques that are specific to their particular roles in the hazardous materials transportation process; and safety, which provides information on hazards posed by materials, proper selection and use of personal protective equipment, and use of emergency respose information.

In addition, driver training is required for highway transportation and motor vehicle operators. Although transporaters will continue to be required to successfuly complete training every year, all others affected by subpart F will be required to receive refresher every two years.

Future of hazardous materials transportation regulations.

The hazardous materials transportation regulations are in a constant state of change, both dometsticaly and internationally. Regulations that are aceptable today may be obsolete tomorrow. Therefore, it is important for all individuals or firrns involved with shipping, receiving, handling, and/or transporting hazardous materials to remain constantly alert to potential regulations changes.

In order to stay up-to-date with the latest changes, an owner/operator should stay in close contact with its transportation company, because the company's managers usually know the upcoming rules changes. Owners/operators are advised to get on transportation industry, vendor, and government mailing lists, because they periodically distribute regulatory updates. Owners/operators can also attend a training course from a reputable trainer at least once every two years. Keeping abreast of the current regulations and changes requires some efort, but the alternative is violating the law.

PCB storage, disposal, and cleanup requirements

Polychlorinated biphenyls present a difficult storage and disposal problem, because the availbale destruction options are severly restricted-namely, to high-temperature incineration at a TSCA permitted facility. Because of the extremely ubiquitous past usage of these compounds, it is worthwhile to examine the unique set of regulations governing PCB storage, disposal, and cleanup practices.

PCBs are specifically regulated under several programs. They are prohibited from discgarge under the toxic pollutant effluent standards of the Clean Water Act and are one of the chemicals regulated under the safe drinking water Act. PCBs are designated hazardous compunds under the comprehensive environmental respones, Comeperhensive Environmental Response, Compensation, and Liability Act and have a reportable quantity of 10 Ib. Most importantly, the Toxic Substance Control Act controls the use of PCBs storage, and disposal requirements, and PCB spill cleanup policy. These regulations are published in 40 CFR 761.

TSCA PCB Regulations

Installation of PCB transformers in or near commercial buildings was banned as of October 1, 1985, except in certain emergency situations or for purposes of reclassification. The U.S. EPA allowed the insytallation of retrofitted PCB transformers until October 1, 1990. the use of lower secondary voltage network PCB transformers located in the sidewalk valuts near commercial buildings was allowed until October 1, 1993.

PCB storage and disposal. PCB articles or PCB containers shall not be stored for longer than one year from the date first placed in storage. In order to comply with storage and disposal requirements, an owner/operator needs to know the concentrations of PCB-contamined articles, items, and liquieds Concentrations of more than 50 parts per millon PCBs are required to be disposed of in a

TSCA-approved facility. Transformers and capacitors are common sources of PCBs.

Expect as noted in 40 CFR 761, PCBs and PCB items must be stored in a facility having all of these characteristics:

- adequate roof and walls to prevent rainwater from reaching stored materials
- adequate floor with 16-in curbing having a containment volume of at least twice the largest PCB article or container
- no drain valves, floor valves, expansion joints, sewer lines, or other openings or conduits
- floors and curbings constructed of smooth impervious materials
- not located below the 100-year floodwater elevation.

All PCB stored materials must be marked with the date that the article was placed in storage, and the storage containers must be checked for leaks at least every 30 days. All PCB storage containers, storage areas, transport equipment, and in-use PCB equipment must be labeled with yellow or white labels as described in 40 CFR 761.40.

Disposal requirements. Disposal of PCBs is carefully regulated under TSCA. PCB-contaminated equipment and/or PCBs at concentrations between 50 and 500 ppm can be disposed in a TSCA-approved incinerator or high-efficiency boiler, or alternatively, in a TSCA-approved chemical waste landfill. Concentrations of PCBs of over 500 ppm require destruction in an approved TSCA incinerator. PCBs and PCB contaminated equipment are required to be manifested, using a serial number or other means of identification. Records of the disposal or destruction are required to be maintained as well as an annual document log of all PCB-related activities. These records are required to be maintained for at least three years after the facility ceases PCB-related activities.

PCB spill cleanup policy

All spills of 10 Ib or more, or spills directly contaminating surface water, sewers, drinking water, grazing lands, or vegetable gardens must be reported to the U.S. EPA regional office within 234 hours after discovery and cleaned up in accordance with measures outlined in 40 CFR 761.125. Also regulated in this section are spills generating PCB concentrations of 50 ppm or greater. In such a case, soils must be remediated to level between 1 and 25 ppm as a function of their actual or anticipated land use, i.e., residential, commercial/industrial.

Cleanup criteria for nonimpervious surfaces are also provide in this section of the regulations. Residential cleanup criteria are considerably more stringent and are based on standard EPA risk assessment methodologies.

Records and monitoring

The operator of a facility storing at one time at least 99.2 Ib of PCBs contained in PCB containers, or one or more PCB transformers, or 50 or more PCB large high-or low-voltage capacitors must develop and maintain records on the storage and disposition of PCBs and PCB items. These records will form the basis of an annual report to be maintained at the storage facility that documents and tracks the disposition of all PCBs and PCB items in storage and disposal.

Water quality

Surface and groundwater quality is regulated through a number of federal and state programs. The Federal Water Pollution Control Act was amended in. 1977 and renamed the clean water act. This act is intended to eliminate the discharge of pollution into navigable waters and to make the nation's waters fishable and swimable. This long-range goal is to be achieved through a combination of industrial discharge regulations, nonpoint source controls, municipal sewage system improvements, and ambient water quality standards. Much of the regulation and implementation of water quality control programs is accomplished through state and/or local governments.

Definitions

The following definitions are relevant to this discussion of water quality:

- *Surface water.* any body of water with its surface exposed to the atmosphere that flows into waters of the United states. U.S. waters are broadly defined to include lakes, rivers, estuaries, washes, bayous, creeks, conduits, irrigation ditches, and-most recently-wetlands.

- *Point source.* a discharge from a specific point or conveyance such as a pipe, drain, conduit, or ditch that directs or funnels discharge water to surface water. Point sources are regulated primarily through
  - — technology-based effluent limitations (how clean the discharge is, using best available control technologies)
  - — permits with local authorities, such as pretreatment standards (pretreatment of wastes prior to discharge to the local publicly owned treatment works)
  - — permits issued under the national Pollutant discharge elimination system for point and nonpoint sources and usually specified limitations on certain constituents.
- *Nonpoint sources.* the 1987 amendments to the CWA give EPA the authority to develop stronger regulations aimed at controlling these secondary or occasional sources of pollution. A nonpoint source is a discharge from an area rather than a specific point. An example of a nonpoint source discharge is contaminated stormwater leaving a facility via overland flow rather than through a specific pipe or point. Soil erosion is another example of a common nonpoint source discharge. nonpoint sources are regulated primarily through water quality management planning and implementation of best management practices.

- *Stormwater*. stormwater run-off can originate from a point source or nonpoint source, depending on the activities storm-inducted water contacts as well as the way it runs off of the property. Stormwater from industrial activity, construction sites, and sources at mining sites is regulated by the state or EPA under the clean water act. the federal regulatory program in 40 CFR 122.26 is implemented through individual, general, or group permits. focus of the regulations is on pollution prevention through implementation of best management practices. Best management practices are delineated in stormwater management plans for facilities. If stormwater and/or process water comes into contact with hazardous or regulated materials and runs off-sits, then this off-site discharge is regulated under the NPDES program.

- *Gròundwater*. Groundwater is water below the land surface in a zone of saturation. There is on umbrella law at the federal level focused on protection of groundwater. Congress has considered various bills aimed specifically at the protection of groundwater supplies; however, as of 1994, none has passed. there are individual state laws and regulations. Most groundwater laws are based on the safe Drinking Water Act of 1974. this law is intended to proved for the safety of drinking water supplies throughout the nation by establishing and enforcing national drinking water quality standards. SDWA regulates the

underground injection of wastewaters and wastes near underground sources of water supplies.

Stormwater regulations: NPDES permits

The U.S. EPA has promulgated final regulations for the water quality act of 1987, which requires that industrial facilities apply for a NPDES permit to cover stormwater discharge. The regulations describing the permit application requirements are given in 40 CFR, part 122.26. The regulations allow for individual industries to submit an application, for group applications for industries that are in the same industrial category, or for industries to be covered under a promulgated general permit. The following describes the classes of facilities that discharge stormwater associated with industrial activity:

- Facilities subject to national effluent limitation guideline.
- Facilities classified as SIC codes 10 through 14, including active and inactive mining and oil and gas operations with contaminated stormwater discharges, except for areas of coal mining operations that have been released by the requirements after 30 days after publication of the final regulation.
- Construction activity (except for disturbances of less than five acres of total land area that are not part of a larger common plan of development or sale).
- Facilities in which materials are exposed to

stormwater classified under SIC codes, 20, 21, 22, 23, 2434, 25, 265, 27, 283, 285, 30, 31, 323, 34, 35, 36, 37, 38, 39, and 4221-25. These codes include food; tobacco; textile; apparel; wood kitchen cabinets; furniture; paperboard containers and boxes; converted paper/paperboard products; printing; drugs' leather; fabricated; metal products' industrial and commercial machinery and computer equipment electronic equipment; transportation equipment; measuring, analyzing, and controlling instruments and photographic, media, and optical goods, and watches and clocks; glass manufacturing, and certain warehousing and storage establishments.

- Vehicle maintenance, equipment cleaning, or airport deicing areas; railroad, mass transit, school bus, trucking, and courier services; postal service; water transportation; airport facilities; and petroleum bulk stations.
- Treatment works treating domestic sewage or any other sewage sludge or wastewaters treatment device or system, used in the storage, treatment, recycling, and reclamation of sewage with a design flow of 1.0 million gallons per day or more are required to have an approved pretreatment program. This does not include farm lands, domestic gardens, or lands used for beneficial refuse of sludge that are not physically located in the confines of the facility.

- Hazardous waste treatment, storage, or disposal facilities.
- Landfills, land application sites, and open dumps that receive industrial.
- Recycling facilities classified as SIC codes 5015 and 5093.
- Steam electric power-generating facilities.

The national policy for the CWA includes providing construction grants for publicly owned treatment works, encouraging technological research, implementing area-wide planning and prohibiting discharge of toxic pollutants in toxicamounts. The impact of the significant CWA amendments in 1977 and subsequent court decisions is to incorporate controls to reduce toxic pollutants. Effluent limitations and guidelines are established for specific industries that discharge waste waters. Water quality programs establish standards and/or controls for toxic chemicals and over 130 priority pollutants.

Sections 301, 304, 306, and 307 of the CWA pertain to technology-based standards for dischargers. These technology-based standards for discharges incorporate industrial direct discharges that require existing sources to use best practice technology by july 1, 1977, regulated by section 301. For new sources more stringent requirements are mandated. The technology based standards for dischargers also require POTWs to use secondary treatment according to local standards.

Other provisions to protect the nation's waters

include EPA's National Ambient Water Quality Criteria promulgated under sections 301, 302, and 303 of the CWA. Clean water was to be achieved by july 1, 1977, through treatment standards and application of technology by industries and POTWs under section 301 of the CWA. The water quality management program objectives directed EPA to assist states in establishing further performance-oriented standards and a system to developed stream segment pollutant load allocation for discharges under Section 303 and 402 of the CWA. It is important to understand that water quality-based standards can dictate discharge limitations fir dischargers more stringently than technology-based standards. Table 8-B lists the mandatory compliance dates for industrial discharges in sections 301 and 307 of the CWA.

Section 402 of the CWA requires a permit from the National Pollutant Discharge elimination System for discharges of pollutants. The NPDES is a regulatory mechanism for permitting point source discharges,. Permit application and/or notice of intent must be filed 180 days prior to discharge of industrial water or stormwater. Point source discharges flow directly into surface waters as opposed to sewer systems. There are different permit applications to file, depending on whether your operation is one of the point source categories with effluent limitations, an existing operation with a permit, or will discharge stormwater only.

To properly manage water quality issues, knowledge of local and EPA environmental compliance guidelines and regulations is a must.

The following list is supplied to assist with the initial phases of identifying permit needs. Further investigation of on-site sewer lines and/or identification of liquid waste sources may be needed after the initial information is revised. This information should be gathered for regulated facilities at a minimum and includes:

- For on-site sewer lines:
  - — List the known discharge points at the facility
  - — Review any construction plans to distinguish between a sanitary sewer and storm sewer lines and discharges.
  - — Inspect areas of sewer discharge inlets.
  - — Inspect the maintenance garage for floor drains and determine their discharge route.
  - — Determine whether there is a local permit for the facility's use of the municipal sewer system. Obtain and review the ordinance or permit regulations.
- For areas of liquid wastes:
  - — Conduct an inspection of facility operation (i.e., vehicle wash area, vehicle parking area, maintenance garage cleanup procedures, storage tank's secondary containment structure).
  - — Identify any liquids or pollutants that may enter the sewer line or be discharged off-

site through a drainage ditch and/or retention pond. These are potential risk areas. Areas of typical pollutants-laden waters are vehicle washwater, liquids from vehicles storing refuse, maintenance garage floor washwater containing oil and grease, antifreeze, hydraulic fluid, motor oil, and transmission fluid leaks.

— Identify the sewer or drain inlet for these liquids or when liquids may drain off-site.

The following conditions include examples of unacceptable releases. Generally, state and federal law prohibit such discharge. The state and local laws and subsequent regulations should be consulted to understand the facility obligations for (1) notifications of discharge to local government treament systems, (2) permit applications for discharges into surface waters, and (3) permit applications for installation of wastewater or treatment systems on site.

Air quality

The clean air act of 1970, as amended, is designed to protect the public health and welfare from the harmful effects of air pollution. Subsequent amendments set definite goals for emission reductions and ambient air quality improvements.

The initial act required the development of primary and secondary national ambient air quality standards and national emission standard foe hazardous air pollutants. Under this act and the amendments states are required to develop state implementation plans 5to implement and enforce these standards. Periodic updates of SUPs are required. In addition, the act's prevention of significant deterioration section prohibits degradation of air quality within classes of air quality regions. The most stringent standards are established for certain pristine areas of the country.

2 Defining Hazardous Wastes

Differentiating hazardous wastes

Given the proper legislative backdrop for management of hazardous wastes, implementation of regulatory control may proceed. The initial task involves the selection of a clear, quantitative means of identifying those wastes that are hazardous. The importance of developing a strong rationale for designating hazardous wastes has often been overlooked, and yet the breadth of the regulatory net is determined by that definition. Subsequently, the economic impact of regulation is directly influenced by the quantities and types of waste that will require special treatment. As is often the case, the magnitude of the economic impact is inversely proportional to the health and environmental impacts being addressed. Thus, implicit with selection of a good definition is identification of the general zone where marginal costs to generators approximate marginal benefits to society.

The primacy of the designation methodology was recognized by Congress when it wrote Section 3001 of RCRA mandating the development of a definitive set of criteria for differentiating hazardous wastes from the rest of the solid waste stream. In route to a discussion of such criteria, it is important to note that numerous other categories of toxic and hazardous materials have been created by legislation in the last decade. A review of the pertinent acts and their intent is therefore instructive.

Two groups of materials are defined in the federal Water Pollution Control Act Amendments of 1972 that are often confused with hazardous wastes: Toxic pollutants and hazardous substances. Toxic pollutants to be designated as result of Section 307 of that act are materials considered to threaten sufficient harm to human health or the environment to warrant specific effluent limitations. These are clearly defined as pure compounds and are designated only in the context of discharges to water.

Therefore, the materials themselves do not constitute hazardous wastes; however, the sludges produced in removing them from liquid streams may be hazardous wastes. Originally, the EPA selected 123 substances foe designation as toxic pollutants. Subsequent litigation resulted in the Flannery decision, a consent decree that was later reinforced by the Clean Water Act of 1977, wherein some 129 "priority pollutants" were designated for control under Section 307. Water quality criteria and industry group effluent guidelines are being developed for each of these contaminates.

Similarly, the Clean Air Act defines a

category of hazardous air pollutants for which the EPA is to promulgate specific emission standards. The capture of these constituents in sludges or some other contained form will subsequently create a hazardous waste.

Hazardous substances are defined in Section 311 of PL 92- 500 as

> such elements and compounds which, when discharged in any quality into or upon the navigable waters of the United States or adjoining shorelines or the waters of the contiguous zone, present an imminent and substantial danger to the public health or welfare, including, but not limited to, fish, shellfish, wildlife, and beaches.

Once again, materials so designated are pure substances and not wastes per se. However, spillage of otherwise designated hazardous wastes may also constitute spillage of hazardous substances based on the pure components included in the waste. In other worlds, hazardous wastes may include hazardous materials as components. Indeed, off-spec or wasted batches of hazardous substances also qualify as hazardous wastes. Conversely, recovered materials after spillage of hazardous substances are likely to constitute hazardous wastes. To date, over 300 elements and compounds have been proposed for designation as hazardous substances.

A related category of legally defined materials that may be confused with hazardous wastes is that addressed by the Toxic Substances Control Act. The enabling legislation provides regulatory options for control of these materials throughout their use and disposal and therefore creates the potential for preemption of hazardous waste regulations. It would appear, however, that Congress intended that hazardous waste regulatory mechanism would prevail once a substance is wasted. The focus of todic substance legislation is production and distribution activities. The intent is to minimize the amounts of unnecessary toxic substances in the marketplace. Consequently, while the legislation affords TSCA regulation throughout the materials existence, for the most part toxic substances become hazardous wastes when discarded.

The interrelation of spilled chemicals and designated hazardous wastes is brought to focus in CERCLA, where hazardous substances are defined as follows:

> "Hazardous substance" means any substance designated pursuant to section 311 of the Federal Water Pollution Control Act; any element, compound, mixture, solution, or substance designated pursuant to Section 102 of this Act, any hazardous waste having the characteristics identified under or listed pursuant to Section 3001 of the Solid Waste Disposal Act, any toxic pollutant listed under Section 307 of the federal Water Pollution Control Act, Any hazardous air pollutant listed under

> Section 112 of the Clean Air Act, and any imminently hazardous chemical substance or mixture with respect to which the administrator has taken action pursuant to Section 7 of the Toxic Substances Control Act. The term does not include petroleum, including crude oil or any fraction thereof which is not otherwise specifically listed or designated as a hazardous substance under subparagraphs through of this paragraph, and the term does not include natural gas, natural gas liquids, liquefied natural gas, or synthetic gas usable for fuel.

Section 102 allows the administrator to add additional entries on the basis of evidence that they may pose a substantial hazard when released in the environment

Given these distinctions, confusion may still occur as a result of the tendency for people to use the terms "Toxic" and "hazardous" interchangeably. The words are not synonymous. The former refers to intrinsic characteristics, whereas the latter also includes extrinsic ones. This distinction has been expressed succinctly by the Food protection Committee of the NAS :

> *Toxic* defines the capacity of the substance to producer injury including effects such as teratogenicity, mutagenicity, and carcinogenicity.

> *Hazardous* denotes the probability that injury will result from use of a substance in a give quantity or manner.

The implications of these definitions may be misleading, because some chemical properties leading to injury are not toxicological in nature. Webster narrows the scope by noting that toxic materials produce injury as a result of poisonous properties. In turn, "poisonous" pertains to injury resulting from chemical action of material via intake or direct contact. In summary, then

"Toxic" refers to an intrinsic property.

"Hazardous" result s from both intrinsic and extrinsic proporties.

"Hazardous" may encompass the potential for injury resulting from toxic *or other* actions.

Having segregated hazardous wastes from other material groups created by legislative action, and having acknowledged the distinction between toxic and hazardous, it is now possible to define hazardous wastes both in generic terms and in a specific quantitative manner.

Defining hazardous wastes

Recognizing that "hazardous" implies both intrinsic and extrinsic factors, any complete definition of hazardous wastes should answer five basic questions:

1. Hazardous to what?
2. Hazardous for what reason

3. Hazardous to that degree?
4. Hazardous at what times?
5. Hazardous under what conditions?

Hazardous to what?

Injury and human can be sustained by a variety of target receptors. Primary concern has typically been associated with human health and property. More recently, attention has also turned to other living organisms and the environment in general. The final factor is somewhat of a catchall that, if taken literally, subsumes the previous three. Whereas in years past, legislative definitions could easily have been restricted to human health, the present atmosphere calls for consideration of all receptors.

Hazardous for what reason?

Once the receptors have been defined, it is necessary to delineate that attributes of the hazard that are to be considered. Candidate attributed include the following.

Ability to bioconcentrate

Toxicity

Flammability

Explosiveness

Reactivity

Irritation or sensitization potential

Corrosivity

Genetic-change potential

Etiology

Radioactivity

Radioactivity often is not considered, because a large body of law and supporting regulations exist to deal with these materials. Radioactivity may also be considered as a subset of toxicity, as can Genetic-change potential. Genetic-change potential and etiology are often grouped in a more general category such as "otherwise damaging" because of vagueness in defining them. Specification of which of these attributes are of concern in th definition of hazardous wastes clearly identifies the types of criteria to be applied in designating specific wastes.

Hazardous to what degree?

In dealing with hazardous wastes, it must be recognized that hazard is not an either or situation, but a matter of degree. That is, hazard for any given material is continuous function dependent on the conditions of exposure. Therefore, some sense of threshold must be established to identify the point at which hazard becomes significant enough to warrant regulation. This can be dealt with qualitatively for definitions that are destined to be included in legislation through use of terms like "substantial" or "significant". A more quantitative treatment is required for a truly working definitions that are destined to be included in quantitative treatment is required for a truly working definition appropriate for regulatory control.

Hazardous at what times?

A definition of hazardous wastes should also address the question of when the hazard is evidenced. This can be viewed in a functional manner, or it can be viewed in a temporal sense. The two views are not completely independent. Handling, transportation, and treatment activities are concerned almost exclusively with present hazards. Storage and disposal activities may involve both present and potential future hazards. Many of the documented incidents involving damage or injury from improper hazardous waste management surfaced some time after storage or disposal was effected. Because damage is not mitigated by the nature of the activity under way at the time, the temporal view appears most appropriate. This assumes that all activities related to the use or management of hazardous wastes fall within the scope of the legislation.

Hazardous under what conditions?

It is important to note the conditions under which the hazard is evidenced. Pertinent factors include quantity, concentration, from, and the presence of other materials that may add to detract from the hazard. These factors are very complicated and consequently difficult to deal with in any but a general manner.

With the passage of the Resource Conservation and Recovery Act of 1976, Congress has created a baseline definition of hazardous wastes answering the foregoing questions:

The term " hazardous waste" means a solid waste, or combination of solid wastes, which because of its quantity, concentration, or physical, chemical, or infectious characteristics may-

(A) cause, or significantly contribute to an increase in mortality or an increase in serious irreversible, or incapacitating reversible illness; or

(B) pose a substantial present or potential hazard to human health or the environment when improperly treated, stored, transported, or disposed of, or otherwise managed.

The definition encompasses a broad scope. In addition to addressing hazards related to physical and chemical properties, it includes infectious hazards and hazards due to the quantity of a waste. On the other hand, the major emphasis is placed on toxicological hazard and especially those hazards evidenced through impacts on th human population. Congress did not list the kinds of specific hazards of concern, nor did Congress choose to designate the hazard level of concern beyond "significant increase" and "substantial present or potential." Hence, the task of quantifying these terms is left to the EPA as an implicit part of Section 30001 regulations.

Finally, the definition focuses on the emergence of these hazards when the waste is improperly managed. This implies certain subtleties not originally a part of hazardous waste designation. Earlier definitions were aimed at segregating wastes that posed these hazards when the wastes were managed along with other nonhazardous solid wastes. The implication was that hazardous wastes had sufficiently different properties that they required special treatment. Hence, in the report to Congress, it was state that.

The term "hazardous waste" means any waste or combination of wastes which pose a substantial present or potential hazard to human health or living organisms because such wastes are lethal, nondegradable, persistent in nature, biologically magnified, or otherwise cause or tend to cause detrimental cumulative effects. General categories of hazardous waste are toxic chemical, flammable, radioactive, explosive, and biological. These wastes can take form of solids, sludges, liquids, or gases.

Withe the RERA terminology, there is greater latitude and consequently more of a burden on the EPA for selecting definitive criteria. All solid waste can cause environmental damage when improperly managed,. The EPA must determines at what point that impact can be defined as a substantial present or potential hazard. Without a listing of the properties of concern, the agency must decide if such impacts as increases in biological oxygen demand, depletion of the ozone layer, corrosiveness, phytotoxicity, or effects on microlife constitute a substantial hazard. Such decisions are key to identification of a proper set of criteria for hazardous waste designation.

Other organizations, such as the National Solid Waste Management Association, have chosen to maintain the posture of the definition in the report to Congress by enumerating the major hazards of concern:

> any waste or combination of wastes which, because of its quantity, concentration, or chemical characteristics, poses a substantial present or potential hazard to human health, living organisms, or the environment because such wastes are bioconcentrative, highly flammable, extremely reactive, toxic, irritating, corrosive, or otherwise damaging.

Similarly, a majority of the state have retained segments describing the primary hazards of interest. Thus, by 1980 35 of the 48 states with formal definitions for hazardous wastes included a listing of hazard types to be addressed. Of the eight states that has adopted the definition in RCRA, two chose to supplement it with a listing of hazards. Eight employed a definition that specified hazardous wastes as those wastes that require special handling or cannot be managed along with "normal" wastes. Although these descriptors are not quantitative, they establish a background philosophy for identifying hazards of concern: Wastes are hazardous if they produce substantial injury to public health or the environment when processes in the same manner as nonhazardous solid wastes. This distinction is not present in the broad RCRA definition, and thus states such as California have developed designation criteria the involve hazards resulting from practices that are not allowed for any wastes, such as direct discharge to rivers or abandonment.

> Toxic and dangerous waste means any waste containing or contaminated by the substances or materials listed in the Annex of this directive of such a nature, or such quantities or in such concentrations as to constitute a risk to health or the environment.

Designating hazardous wastes

The process of designating hazardous wastes is difficult and ultimately involves some of the classic trade-offs encountered in environmental regulation, such as that between ease of implementation and equity between parties. As in the case with selection of a generic definition, there is no single right way to designate hazardous wastes. There are good and bad ways to accomplish designation, based on the primary concerns of the community.

To date, two basic approaches to designation have been developed: listing and use of criteria thresholds for intrinsic waste properties. Each approach offers advantages that must be weighed against inherent weaknesses.

Listing

Designation of hazardous wastes though listing was one of the first options explored by the EPA and its contractors. In this approach, candidate waste streams are reviewed by source and segregated into hazardous and nonhazardous categories. Those deemed to be hazardous are then so designated generically. Hence, if selected drilling muds are assessed to be hazardous, drilling muds in general are listed as hazardous. This process is continued until all hazardous waste source streams have been identified, evaluated, and listed.

The major advantage of this approach is its ease of implementation and enforcement. Once wastes have been designated, all wastes can readily be categorized by source. Both generators regulators can quickly determine the status of a waste. No testing is required. As a consequence, costs associated with identification of hazardous wastes are low.

This ease of implementation is gained at the expense of equitable treatment and technical correctness. Categorization by source ignores the reality that waste streams from two generically similar sources may have greatly different properties. The use of different additives, varying process conditions, and postprocess treatment can significantly change the nature of a waste. Generic designation by source fails to recognize these differences and ultimately stands as a disincentive to the generator who may modify his process to reduce the hazardousness of his waste.

The listing approach is also quite limiting in that it does not accommodate new wastes or combination of wastes. The list of designated wastes is current at a point in time when the evaluation is made. From that point forward, it is outdated as new processes and new products continue to changes the nature and number of candidate waste streams. As a consequence, an updating schedule is required, with periodic evaluation of wastes to reaffirm or change designations.

Listing approach have been relatively common in the European community. The proposed bill for a special chemical waste act in. The Netherlands called for a listing of names of substances that would be addressed in an order of council. Subsequently, wastes have been categorized and threshold concentrations specified. A federal-state committee on disposal of special refuse in West Germany has produced a lost of 35 types of waste that cannot be disposed with municipal waste. Similarly, by 1970 Denmark had listed 39 process wastes and classes of chemicals as hazardous. In the United Kingdom, the Greater? London Council, which administers the Deposit of Poisonous Waste Act in that geographic area, utilizes a classification system identifying wastes by constituents. Similarly, Japan has defined hazardous wastes as those including one or more of the following constituents: alkyl mercury, mercury and its compounds, cadmium and its compounds, lead and its compounds, organic phosphorous compounds, chromium VI compounds, arsenic and its compounds, cyanides, and polychlorinated biphenyls.

The first implementation of a listing approach in the United States took place in California pursuant to the California Hazardous

Waste Control Act of 1973. Prior to the amendments of 1977, this act required that the Department of Health "shall prepare, adopt, and may revise when appropriate, a listing of the wastes which are determined to be hazardous".

The list of hazardous wastes and the list of extremely hazardous wastes adopted by the Department have been extensively revised and will be heard publicly and adopted in the next few months. Since the law requires the Department to adopt these lists, proposed revisions must be subjected to public hearings. Due to new materials being developed as well as others being discontinued, it is virtually impossible to maintain an up-to-date list.

To prevent this, Dr. Collins recommended that other states should authorize agencies to develop and maintain lists without adopting the lists themselves are regulations. This would not circumvent the need for continual updating, but it would eliminate costly public hearings and the time delays associated with a formal regulatory change. Because this option was not available in california, the department included with the the generic listing several blanket clauses that give greater flexibility to testing: (1) the waste contains substances listed in Articles 2 and 3 of the attached regulations, or (2) the waste contains substances known to be hazardous or extremely hazardous and defined in Sections 25117 and 25115, respectively, of the attached hazardous waste law.

The first of these constitutes a second kind of listing approach for designation of hazardous wastes: the pure compound approach. The pure compound approach emerged during the development of the report to Congress. It is predicated on the assumption that the hazardous properties of a waste stream will be those of the most hazardous constituent. Therefore, a list of hazardous chemicals is developed, and wastes found to contain any of these are subsequently designated hazardous.

Candidate constituents for use in the pure compound approach may be selected in a number of ways. To data, lists have been generated through collection of lists designated hazardous by other agencies, e.g., DOE and USDA. Lists may also be generated by applying hazard criteria on thresholds and determining which chemicals exceed these numeric values. A third way to generate lists as well as a means of putting lists in perspective is to review the constituents which have been implicated in hazardous waste incidents in the past.

The advantage of the pure compound approach is that data on most of the selected hazardous chemicals are much more readily available than data on waste streams. Therefore, literature data can be employed and waste analysis reduced to chemical characterization. This eliminates costly hazards testing of waste streams. Conversely, reliance on published chemical data is also the major weakness of the pure compound approach. Assigning the properties of a single constituent to a complex waste mixture fails to account for interactions between constituents that may markedly alter the hazardous nature of a waste. Such interactions can include the following.

Additive effects, where constituents operate through similar mechanisms and thereby stress the receptors as if they were the same total quantity of just one of the constituents

Synergistic effects, where the total effect of a combination of constituents is greater than the sum of their individual effects (example would be the mixture of chlorinated hydrocarbon pesticides and solvents, and cadmium and zinc in water)

Antagonistic effects, the functional opposite of synergistic effects, where the total effect is less than the sum of effects of the constituents

Chemical interaction effects, where the presence of one constituent modifies the hazard potential of another through direct chemical reaction or modifies the availability of that constituent to the receptor.

Similarly, a mixture of non hazardous constituents may react to produce a hazardous product in the waste stream. These shortcomings can be resolved only by direct hazard testing of waste stream.

A second major weakness in both the pure compound approach and the listing by source approach is a subtle one that becomes visible upon comparison to the criteria approach. In the evaluation for selection of generic waste streams or hazardous constituents, it is necessary to establish some means of measurement, some criteria by which candidates are determined to qualify as hazardous. For equity and resolution, these criteria should be quantitative. If regulators rely in existing lists of hazardous chemicals, they are tacitly excepting someone else's criteria developed for different purpose. If a new set of criteria are developed, then, in essence, a criteria approach has been taken. However, the equitable treatment of the latter has been foregone to avoid the costs of waste stream hazard testing.

The state of Washington has developed a scheme to accommodate many of the advantages of the two systems in the context of a criteria approach. This methods is described in the following section. Recognizing the inherent difficulties in relaying solely on a listing approach to designation, most states have gone to alternative systems. the 1977 amendments to the California Hazardous Waste Disposal Act added the requirement for adoption by regulation of "criteria and guidelines for the identification of hazardous wastes and extremely hazardous wastes." Similarly, RCRA requires the EPA to "promulgate criteria for identifying the characteristics of hazardous wastes and for listing hazardous waste."

As such, the listing approach is evolving as a part of the designation procedure that can be employed in one of two ways:

1. List are provided as the designation mechanism, but their constituency is determined through the application of criteria.
2. List are employed merely as wa convenience to generators and administrators, indicating which wastes would be subjected to direct hazard testing prior to designation.

Criteria

The criteria approach to designation of hazardous wastes is a quantitative one that be applied directly to wastes or to chemical for selection of entries in a pure compound approach. The methodology relies on comparison of specific material characteristics to a selected threshold value. When the threshold is exceeded, the material is designated as hazardous. For example, one could define as hazardous all wastes with a flash point of 100 F or less. One selected, any constituent or waste stream could be evaluated for designation against this threshold. Values for comparison can be measured empirically or calculated from component data.

Use of criteria eliminates many of the weakness associated with listing approaches. The criteria can be applied to any future waste as well as those currently being generated. hence, there is a mechanism for continual updating without the need for regulatory change or public hearings. Once the criteria have been accepted through the public hearing and comment process, wastes pass or fail based on intrinsic properties. Legal challenges and adversarial proceedings are minimized. Criteria and associated testing procedures are published so that generators, shippers, public officials, and disposal site operators as well as regulators can evaluate any given waste to determine its proper designation.

As suggested previously, the major weakness of the criteria approach is the cost and time associated with testing waste streams directly. Toxicological and physical testing can require significant expenditure, depending upon the number and type of tests involved. Single-dose screening bioassays may be accomplished for as little as $1000 per sample. Chronic and sublethal or genetic activity tests could exceed $ 500,000 for a single material.

Following recognition of the impact of these potential costs, additional mechanisms have been devised to minimize testing and to leave the decision whether or not to test to the generator who will bear the cost. A common means of minimizing testing is to offer a listing approach on an advisory basis. List are provided indicating that all waste streams enumerated should be treated as hazardous unless the generate wished to test them and in so doing show that they do not meet criteria. The generator can weight the cost of testing against the cost differential for available disposal options and make the decision to test or not test on an economic basis.

A second methodology has been devised as an intermediate measure between application of advisory waste listings and direct waste testing.

In this case, formulations are provided to allow the generator to calculate hazardous property parameters utilizing data on the waste's components. The derived values are then compared to modified thresholds are conservatively selected to provide for a safety margin, because calculated valued do not take into account any of the possible interactions between constituents. An example of calculated guidelines can be found in an early draft of the proposed California regulations.

Utilizing these intermediate steps, a generator can schedule evaluation activities to minimize expenditures. If his waste is listed in a guideline list, he can calculate thresholds to determine the accuracy of the designation list. If he fails the calculated test, he may proceed to a direct waste stream test. At each point he has the opportunity to make an economic trade-off analysis between the costs of proceeding and the benefits to having waste designated nonhazardous. The cost-conscious generator will also prioritize the parameters he evaluated from least costly tests to more expensive ones. In so doing, if he fails a criteria associated by less expensive tests, he need not proceed with more costly tests for other hazard parameters.

Application of a criteria approach requires two types of selection activity: selection of hazardous parameters of concern and selection of threshold values for those parameters.

Although damage classification does not

desegregate data to individual hazard types or receptor categories, some general conclusions can be drawn. For one thing, water is most often affected as the transport medium and groundwater problems suggests further that effects on potable water are major concerns. This is borne out by complementary data revealing that as a result of these 421 cases, 140 wells were affected. Following this conclusion, the EPA draft criteria for defining hazardous wastes have narrowed toxicity criteria to this: the presence of constituents that form a leachate with contaminant concentrations equal to or greater than 10 times drinking water standards. No provisions are made for aquatic toxicity, phytotoxicity or inhalation toxicity or for the numerous chemicals that have not been incorporated in drinking water standards.

This is a considerable deviation from the position taken in the report to Congress. At the time, the EPA offered a preliminary criteria system described as the "hazardous waste decision model", which included 11 hazard categories for evaluation. This more expansive view of the breadth of hazards to be considered has been carried forward by individual states. Of the 35 states they by 1980 had employed a hazard listing of some kind in the generic definition of hazardous waste, the frequencies of occurrence for individual hazards were as follows:

Toxic 30

Explosive 28

Infectious 24

Radioactive 21

Flammable 17

Corrosive 17

Irritant 10

Bioconcentrative 10

Genetically active 3

Reactive 2

These data can be somewhat misleading as a result of the impreciseness of terms employed. Some states assume that "toxic" covers a spectrum of discrete hazards such as "bioaccumulative " and "genetically active", just as "explosive" and "reactive" and "corrosive" and "irritant" may be somewhat synonymous. In developing quantitative criteria, the toxic category is often broken down further to cover oral, dermal, inhalation, and aquatic toxicity. Before reviewing the threshold values that have been selected for designation criteria, a brief discussion of each hazard type will be instructive.

Toxicity

Toxicity is the ability of a waste to produce injury upon contact with a susceptible site in or one the body of a living organism. Toxicity hazard is the risk that injury will be caused by the manner in which a waste is handled. Wastes may be acutely or chronically hazardous to pants or animals via a number of routes of administration. Phytotoxic wastes can damage plants when present in the soil, atmosphere, or irrigation water. Phytotoxicity is the result of a reduction of chlorophyll production capability, overall growth retardation, or some specific chemical interference mechanism.

Wastes that are acutely toxic to mammals may be active when inhaled, ingested, and/or contacted with the skin. Acute effects are genrally evidenced within hours of inhalation or after a single dermal or oral dose. Data pertinent to a single route of administration may not be applicable to alternative in the air, but in water asbestos particles may not pose an ingestive threat at low levels.

Wastes may be chronically toxic to mammals if they contain materials that (1) are bioaccumulated or concentrated in the food chain or (2) cause irreversible damage that builds gradually to a final, unacceptable level. Classic examples of chronic toxicants are the heavy metals and halogenated aromatic compounds. Wastes can also be highly toxic to aquatic organisms. Much data exist on the effects of various materials on fish and fish food organisms.

Because of the various routes of exposure that may ultimately lead to hazardous effects, toxicity must be viewed as a function of the transport medium, the physical characteristics of the waste, and the type of disposal practices involved. Although water is perhaps the most pervasive vector, atmospheric emission s may well faster and spread farther. Direct contact is the most easily controlled route of exposure.

Toxic wastes can be derived from practically any industry. Toxicity may be the result of pure constituents within the stream, the total effects of several similar waste stream components, or the combined actions of two individually nontoxic materials.

Acute toxicity is typically measured through use of an LD_{50} or an LC_{50}. These terms refer to the median lethal does and the median lethal concentration, respectively. They are quantitative measures of the dose at which 50% of a test population will die from exposure to a chemical under prescribed conditions. For oral and dermal contract, a single dose is administered, and the test subjects are observed for 14 days. For inhalation, the test animal my be exposed continuously or periods of up to eight or more hours. Similarly, phytotoxicity and aquatic toxicity tests are conducted continuously for a prescribed period. A test period of 96 has become quire standard for the latter test and is often described as the indicator of acute effects as opposed to chronic effects. chronic toxicity measurements are not nearly as standardized.

Explosiveness and Reactivity

Explosive wastes may be detonated by several mechanisms: thermal shock, mechanical shock, electrostatic charge, or contact with incompatible materials. Like flammable wastes, highly reactive ones may threaten life and property in an acute sense and a latent sense in that the detonation may occur before or after "disposal". In the first case, handling, shipment, or disposal operations can initiate violent reactions, resulting in an explosion. In the second case, reactive materials may be burried in a landfill and, like a time bomb, await the appropriate conditions for detonation.

Typically, the kill radius for explosive wastes will be less than that for comparable volumes of flammable liquids. Prior experience with transportation related explosions indicates a casualty raidus of 100-200 ft. Detonation of a single waste may be followed by secondary explosions of fire. The magnitude of the hazard existing after completion of disposal activities may exceed the handling hazard if sufficient waste inventory is accumulated.

Reactive wastes include explosive manufacturing wastes, contaminated industrial gases, and old ordnance. There is no universal property of reactivity that allows a single quantitative scale for categorizing these materials. Mechanical-shock-sensitive materials may be described by results of a drop test, such as that associated with the Picatinny Arsenal scale. Other types of reactive materials are simply classified using narrative descriptions. The most common rating is done developed by the NFPA. This system divides materials into five categories, 0-4, based on the degree of hazard anticipated in handling them. The extreme hazard group includes the following:

Materials that can be detonated by elctrostatic charge

Oxidizing materials such as chlorates,

perchlorates, bromates, peroxides, nitrates, and permanganates

Self-reactive materials

Materials capable of autopolymerization

Primary explosives than may be detonated by friction, impact, shock , or heat (rated 5 inches or less on the Picatinny Arsenal Scale)

Materials that react violently with air or water

The National Academy of Sciences has also created a classification system for characterizing the reactivates of chemicals with themselves, water, and other chemicals. Grade 4 materials may react with otherwise nonreacting materials, may react vigorously with water, on may undergo self-oxidation.

Infectiousness

Infectious wastes are those materials that contain disease-causing organisms or matter. Pathogenic waste are those containing organisms, bacteria, or virus that may cause disease. Although infectious and pathogenic waste have been excluded from the purview of this text, it must be recognized that this hazard type is one of the most frequently listed concerns in generic definitions of hazardous wastes. Wastes that are infectious or contain infectious materials pose a hazard to handlers and the public if they are not isolated and/ or disposed of in a manner that destroys the viability of the infectious matter. At the same time, it is recognized that infectious organisms are ubiquitous in the environment and thus are present at varying levels in all manner of materials. This is particularly true of wastes such as sewage sludges and municipal refuse. Therefore, it is necessary to define criteria carefully such that virtually all wastes do not fall subjects to hazardous waste regulation. Two approaches have been attempted in the past.

1. Exempt specific wastes such as sewage sludges.
2. Use the sources as a part of the criterion.

Options for the latter approach would, for instance, designate as hazardous all infectious wastes resulting from medical experimentation or from diagmnosis, care, or treatment of diseased humans or animals. These would include the following.

(1) Laboratory waste such as pathological specimens, infectious cultures, and disposable fomites.

2. Surgical and obsterical wastes such as pathological specimens and disposable fomites

3 Equipment, instruments, utensils, and fomites of a disposable nature from the room of patients or subjects with suspected or diagnosed communicable disease.

For the purpose of the foregoing, pathological specimens include tissues and specimens of blood elements, excreta, and secretions obtained from patients or subjects. Infectious cultures include those used for detection, maintenance, or isolation of infectious organisms or suspected infectious organisms, such as microorganisms and helminths capable of producing infection or infectious disease. Fomites include any substance that may harbor or transmit infectious organisms.

Aside from the operational wastes described earlier, this category would also cover such special wastes as carcasses from livestock epidemics and materials from biological warfare agents. As written, it would not include wastes such as dead limbs from trees affected by Dutch elm blight, and yet these wastes may also pose an infectious threat and have required special treatment in the past.

Whereas the use of source-derived criteria for designating infectious wastes has been widely accepted, it should be noted that many states supplement criteria with an exemption for sewage sludges. This is often based on an economic decision because of the large volumes of material involved and the higher costs of hazardous waste disposal. Tacit in this exception is the belief that the infectious hazard can be reduced or eliminated with standard procedures used at the sewage treatment plant. For instance, many pathogenic organisms are destroyed with anaerobic digestion. On the other hand, parasites such as *Ascaris* are not. It is also important to note that sewage sludges may well meet other hazardous waste criteria such as those related to the presence of heavy metals and toxic chemicals. Therefore, when sewage sludges are to be exempted, the exemption should be accompanied by regulations that assure proper treatment and disposal of these materials outside hazardous waste management regulations.

Radioactivity

Radioactive materials have been intentionally deleted from the scope of the technical discussions of this text. This reflects the fact that radioactive waste management is a technology of its own that could easily fill several volumes. It aslo recognizes that these materials are, for the most part, addressed by the Atomic Energy Act of 1954 as amended and therefore are regulated by the Nuclear Regulatory Commission. A caution is warranted, here, however. The 1054 Act is not inclusive for all radioactive materials. The EPA has the authority to regulate releases of such materials as radium and isotopes produced in accelerators. Therefore, there is a limited gap in regulatory control that some states have chosen to cover through hazardous waste regulation.

Ionizing radiation results from an instability of the nucleus of an atom. The drive towards stability causes a radioactive release that may be manifested in one of many forms. The four major types of radiation are the following:

1. Alpha particles consist of two protons and two neutrons and are the largest and heaviest of the emissions. Interaction with orbital electrons slows alpha particles considerably, an thus they do not travel more that 3 inches when emitted in air. Consequently, they are incapable of penetrating the dead outer layer of human skin. However, ingestion, inhalation,

or adsorption of alpha emitters can be extremely hazardous because of their potential ability to damage internal organs unprotected by epidermal layers. elements with an atomic number of 84 or greater are typical alpha emitters.

2. Beta particles are electrons emitted at high speeds. Their small size and great velocity allows beta particles to travel as far as 10-100 ft in air, and yet can penetrate human skin burns, and internal doses can be highly hazardous even at very low levels. Effects include debilitation of reproductive capability and injury to specific organs.

3. Gamma radiation is electromagnetic energy rather than matter. In contrast to alpha radiation, gamma radiation poses and extreme external as well as internal exposure hazard because of its ability to travel great distances and deeply penetrate human tissue. Gamma rays may not be as hazardous when present internally because of their ability to exit the body without colliding with electrons and causing damage. Many radioisotopes of common elements are gamma emitters.

4. Neutrons separated from the nucleus and traveling at very high speeds constitute a fourth form of radiation. Although human exposure is rare, it is extremely dangerous because of tissue-penetrating capabilities exceeding several feet.

Several major health hazards may result from exposure to radiation: (1) large acute external doses may result in burns or damage to internal organs; (2) large acute internal does may result in damage to internal organs; (3) low-level chronic internal doses may accumulate in the body until toxic action results; (4) radiation can interfere with the normal; functioning of the nuclei of human cells, leading to malignancy; and (5) irradiation of reproductive organs can lead to sterility or possibly harmful mutations.

Wastes containing radioactive materials may cause any or all of the foregoing effects. Acute exposure can result from impropermandling by employees or improper disposal to nonsecured locations. Chronic exposure can potentially result from leaching of landfills, volatilization of radioactive materials, or proximity to unmarked repositories.

Radioactive wastes can be categorized by activity level (the rate at which the nucleus of the isotope decays) and therefore are subject to quantitative characterization. Relative safe levels have been defined as maximum permissible concentrations, which can be used as a point of reference for designating wastes as hazardous.

Flammability

Highly flammable wastes can pose both acute handling hazards and latent disposal hazards. Handling problems involve safety hazards to personnel at the site of origin, during transport, and at the disposal site. An example of a latent disposal hazard is the potential damage caused by uninternational or spontaneous combustion of flammable residues at a disposal site Fear of such consequences has led to a ban on landfilling of flammable liquids in many areas.

Both acute and latent hazards relate to injury, destruction of property, and/or rapid depletion of resources. A 9,000-gal tank truck and a 30,000-gal tank car of flammable liquid are likely to be associated with kill radii of 115 and 230 ft, respectively, if ignited during handling or transport operations. Secondary effects beyond the initial disaster area may include ignition of nearby inflammables and detonation of hear-sensitive substances in the vicinity. Hazards relate to disposal site may exceed those of transpiration and handling if sufficient waste volumes are involved. Flammable wastes may include contaminated solvents, oils, pesticides, plasticizers, complex organic sludges, and off-specification chemicals.

Flammable wastes may be characterized for relative categorization or compared on the basis of flammability properties. Properties typically measured as an indication of material flammability include flash point and autoignition temperature.

Flash points is defined as the minimum temperature at which a liquid will give off sufficient vapor to form and ignitable mixture in the air above the liquid's surface. An ignitable mixture in this context is a vapor air mixture within the flammable range. Some solids such as camphor and naphthalene volatilize sufficiently to have flash points, but the measure refers most directly to liquids. Flash point is measured by standard analytical techniques wherein an ignition sources is used to determine when the vapor air mixture is in fact ignitable. Flash point should not be confused with fire point. The latter is the temperature at which a liquid can sustain combustion. It is genrally several degrees higher than the flash point, because additional heat is required to sustain the vapor- air mixture in the flammable range over time.

The autoignition temperature is the minimum point at which a material will self-ignite. This measure is highly sensitive to the conditions under which the test is run and therefore does not represent a universal value for a material. As a consequence, autoignition temperature has not received as much use as flash point.

The most widely accepted scheme for categorization of flammable materials is that employed by the National Fire Protection Association. This classification system includes five groupings, 0-4, similar to the reactivity groupings. Placement in a group is based on a combination of properties. The most flammable materials, category 4, are characterized as "very flammable gases, very volatile flammable liquids, and materials that in the form of dusts or mists readily from explosive mixtures when dispersed in air."

Actual categorization of specific materials has been based on judgment of a reviewing committee. In general, category 4 materials are in one of the following categories;

1. Flammable gases
2. Flammable liquids with boiling points below 100°F and vapor densities ≥1.1 (density is measured as the ratio of the weight of a volume of vapor, to an equal volume of dry air under similar conditions)
3. Flammable liquids with flash points below 100 F and vapor- air densities ≥1.1.
4. Materials spontaneously combustible in air

The vapor and vapor-air density data are meant to account for the hazard of vapors travelling along the ground to an ignition source and then flashing back. This could be a real hazard in landfill operations, where heavy equipment exhaust or sparks could ignite escaping vapors.

Corrosiveness

Corrosiveness is defined as the ability of one agent to eat away or erode another material through chemical action. The reactor material may be biological membranes. However, this action is generally addressed with criteria for irritation. Therefore, corrosiveness in this context refers to action on inanimate materials. Therefore, corrosiveness in this context refers to action on inanimate materials. The hazard posed by corrosive materials is largely evidenced during handling and storage activities when containment may be breached. This can result both in release of the corrosive material itself and in the opportunity for these materials to release other hazardous wastes such as pyroforic, toxic, or explosive materials. Some concern has also been expressed with respect to the ability of corrosive materials to solubilize otherwise immobile heavy metals.

The desirability of considering corrosive properties in hazardous waste designation has been a point of contention during the regulatory development period. The hazard posed during handling and storage is already addressed by OSHA and DOT rules and guidelines. Indeed, DOT standards are often employed for selecting corrosive criteria. Hence, inclusion for these concerns constitutes an area of overlap. Consideration on the grounds that these materials may be disposed in metal drums is a moot point, because drum corrosion will occur over time regardless of the contents. Corrosive materials will merely accelerate this natural process. If the concern is focused on release of contents in a landfill, that concern is misplaced. Drums are not an effective barrier to release in the landfill environment. Indeed, the use of drums during waste disposal is a practice designated to facilitate loading, transport, unloading, and placement through temporary containment. As a consequence, the decision for including corrosiveness as a hazard of concern rests with the appraisal of the adequacy of existing regulation for storing and transporting these materials and concerns for solubilization of metals.

Corrosiveness is most often measured in terms of the material's ability to corrode a given thickness of steel during a set period of time. Corrosiveness is also often associated with acidity or alkalinity. Subsequent criteria can therefore be defined on the basis of pH. Both of these measures are quantitative and accommodate selection of a criteria threshold.

Irritation

Some wastes (namely, those containing allergens capable of sensitizing skin, agents that cause contact dermatitis, or substances that are corrosive to living tissues) can cause severe discomfort if contacted. Examples of these wastes are concentrated acids and alkalis, waste warfare agents, and waste substances with allergenic properties. Such wastes pose a hazard when discharged to waterways or uncontrolled landfills where accidental exposure cannot be prevented.

When the primary irritant response of a material can be traced to acidity or alkalinity, pH can be employed as a quantitative measure for criteria comparison. Similar measurements are more difficult for non-acid-mediated irritation and sensitization. In the latter case, designation is made by definition. Materials are classified as sensitizers if contact with them is found to render the receptor more susceptible to allergic reactions on future exposures or on exposure to other materials. Some materials are also photosensitizers. In this case, the receptor becomes sensitized to exposure to light of wavelengths between 280 and 430 nm.

For materials that irritate eyes or skin but are not adequately characterized with pH measurement, arbitrary scales have been devised to connote relative irritant power. The FDA methodology employes a 10-point ordinal scale with values assigned based on the severity of dermal response. Higher, more hazardous ratings are associated with moderate or severe edema and erythema after 24-h exposure. A second system available for quantifying irritant capability has been devised by Smyth and co-workers. With this approach, specific dermal responses are observed at varying chemical concentrations and are assigned grades accordingly. For instance, grade 8 categorizes materials that produce necrosis (death or decay of tissue) when applied in a 1% soultion. Grade 10 materials produce a similar response when applied in a 0.01% solution.

Bioconcentration

The term "bioconcentration" is used to describe the hazard posed by materials that can be concentrated in a single organism or magnified by successive levels in the food chain until they reach toxic levels. The hazard is one of chronic exposure, and it generally occurs when the contaminant is present in the environment at low levels.

Wastes may possess this characteristic as a result of the presence of bioconcentrative constituents such as cadmium, lead, mercury, polychlorinated biphenyls, or carbon tetrachloride. Improper disposal of these wastes can lead to release of low levels of bioconcentrative materials to the environment. Organisms may then pick up and concentrate these materials until concentration reaches a sufficient level to cause death or debility. Concentration to the threshold toxic level often occurs in higher life forms such as fish, birds, and mammals, including man. this hazard may be evidenced in hazardous waste management as a result of long-term disposal to productive surface waters or through landfarming where crops are ultimately employed for consumption.

Bioconcentration factors are defined as the ratio of the concentration of the contaminant in an organism to the concentration of that contaminant in the surrounding environment or food. The definition is not relevant to materials with cumulative effects or materials for which substantial nutritional requirements have been established. In general, bioconcentrated materials as defined here are those for which the detoxification-excretion mechanism is either nonexistent or extremely slow.

Bioconcentrative materials can be grouped into two categories, based on retention mechanisms. The first includes the heavy metals, such as mercury and lead. These materials, through a strong affinity characteristic with sulfhydryl groups and disulfide bonds, are capable of inactivating or denaturing enzymes and proteins, thus blocking normal metabolic pathways, interfering with control mechanisms, and crippling cellular integrity. The second category of bioconcentrative substances is represented by persistent organic materials such as DDT and PCBs. These materials concentrate through an affinity for nonpolar solvents and low solubility in water. The contaminants quickly migrate to fatty tissues or lipid cellular fractions, where they typically cause hepatic disorders.

Evaluating the data on bioconcentration can be very difficult, because no standard bioassay or testing procedure has been adopted by which the bioconcentration potential of a material can be consistently assessed. One alternative proposed for selection of bioconcentrative materials is response to octanol-water partition tests. Others rely on analysis of residuals in model environment studies. Until such a standard testing procedure is developed, literature sources documenting environmental buildup of a material or laboratory studies indicating less than complete elimination or detoxification of a material by one of the higher organisms of animal life must be used to select substances under this criterion.

Genetic activity

Wastes may contain materials with carcinogenic, mutagenic, or teratogenic properties, evidenced as malfunctions of the genetic process either in mitosis or meiosis. When chemically induced, such effects may be the result of chemical modification of DNA nucleotides in the target species. Exposure routes are usually direct and continuous.

Dye plant wastes and petroleum sludges can contain genetically active materials. The California Hazardous Wastes Working Group noted that:

> Most proofs of carcinogenesis in humans are limited to occupational exposures but there is probably a general population exposure of unknown magnitude. Various reports substantiate this assumption in one way or another and give emphasis to the urgent need for comprehensive chemical, experimental, and epidemiologic studies to determine actual hazards.

More recent estimates of "environmentally" induced cancer range from 60% to 90% of all cancer cases. Hence the concern for releases of materials with even low levels of known or probable carcinogens.

Knowledge of genetic activity is currently such that numeric values or rating systems have not been devised to quantitatively compare potencies or assess risk. In part, this reflects fundamental disagreement among experts as to the nature of the hazard. A primary facet of the controversy rests with the existence or nonexistence of threshold concentrations for chemically induced carcinogenesis. These are the opposing views:

Chemical carcinogenesis, like radiologically induced cancer,is a function of probability upon exposure; i.e., with each exposure there is a given statistical chance for a carcinogenic response. Hence, even a single exposure increases the probability of response, and all exposure is to be avoided regardless of concentration. On the basis of this assumption, chemicals can be assigned a cancer risk value which can be compared between chemicals to rank potency.

Chemical carcinogenesis is directly related to the degree of exposure only for materials above a set concentration threshold. Hence, low-level exposures are of no consequence, and safety standards, potency ratings, and categorization can be based on the numeric value of the threshold.

Belief that there may be no measurable threshold for carcinogens has fostered responses such as the Delaney clause, which forbids the addition of any known carcinogenic material to food products in any concentration.

Without accepted numeric ratings for genetic activity, criteria have of necessity followed the lines of the pure constituent approach. That is, wastes are defined as genetically active if they contain known carcinogens, teratogens, or mutagens above a given concentration. Selection of the threshold concentration is highly controversial because of the considerations previously noted. There is also a great deal of controversy over what data are required to declare a constituent a known carcinogen. Standard tests have been and continue to be developed and endorsed by such groups as the National Cancer Institute, but the interpretation of results continues to rely heavily on the judgment of the evaluator.

Extraction procedures

Extraction procedures have long been employed as a means of dissolving and/or separating complex materials for the purposes of analysis. In solid and hazardous waste management, extraction procedures take on added importance, because they are employed to simulate leachate generation and therefore provide a basis for prediction of mobility after disposal. It is this predictive aspect of extraction procedures that has aroused controversy with respect to use in regulatory definition for segregating hazardous and non-hazardous wastes. Because of the added costs associated with the management of wastes classified as hazardous, generators of waste are concerned about the degree to which any given procedure represents what will happen in the disposal environment.

Extraction procedures employed for differentiating hazardous and non-hazardous wastes have four major elements; (1) specification of how the waste is prepared for the evaluation, (2) specification of the solution used for leaching, (3) specification of the means and extent of contact, and (4) specification of how resulting extracts are to be analyzed. The first three of these factors are reviewed next. Issues related to analysis are left to other texts.

Waste preparation

The rate of leaching is directly related to the surface area of the material being leached. As a consequence, the degree to which a waste is reduced in size will greatly affect the result of an extraction procedure. The EPA extraction procedure calls for the use of a sample that has a surface area 3.1 cm or passes through a 9.5-mm standard sieve, while California has proposed a threshold particle size associated with passage through a #10 sieve.

At issue with respect to sample preparation is the degree to which size reduction may discourage the fixation of wastes. Fixation processes may involve materials that encapsulate and physically entrap contaminants rather than chemically binding them. In these cases, size reduction will breach the coating and allow leach solutions to reach otherwise contained contaminants. As such, extraction will be much higher than can be anticipated from typical disposal site conditions, where the fixed mass is not likely to be broken down to smaller sizes as a result of weathering and other natural forces. To circumvent these problems, it has been recommended that size reduction be applied only to those wastes that fail a specified structural integrity test. Wastes that pass can be evaluated in a monolithic from.

Leachate solution selection

Once the sample is prepared, it is exposed to the leach solution in order to initiate extraction. The chemistry of the solution can greatly affect subsequent leaching. For instance, low-pH solutions are likely to solubilize metal salts, and alkaline waters will produce higher concentrations of certain organic chemicals. Similarly, the presence of chelating agents will sponsor increased mobility of metals and other contaminants through complexation. In the simple case of disposal of a single waste at a given site, the leachate can be made to simulate rainwater through use of distilled water. Somewhat higher acidity may be desirable to simulate acid rainfall conditions encountered in more industrialized areas. Where codisposal with organic-based wastes is anticipated, more sophisticated solutions are employed. These "synthetic garbage juices" are mixed to simulate the organic acids derived during anaerobic decomposition of refuse. A typical formulation calls for use of acetic acid or sodium acetate, and some states have gone to more active ingredients . For instance, the state of California employs citrate, a stronger complexant than acetate.

A great deal of controversy surrounds the selection of the leachate solution. Industrial commentators have been highly critical of the EPA for using acetate, which is known to free up metals and other toxic chemicals. They propose distilled water as a compromise to the "worst-case" scenario. Other observers support the use of both distilled water and acetate to provide categorization of wastes. Those failing criteria with an acetate leach but passing with distilled water would be restricted to noncodisposal landfilling options; i.e., these wastes would be segregated from an environment where acetate or other organic acid constituents would be anticipated.

The effect of employing different leach solution has been investigated in recent work sponsored by the EPA. A number of proposed extract solutions were employed in parallel studies on five industrial wastes; dewatered sludge from a POTW, organic still bottoms, ink pigment waste, baghouse dust, and pharmaceutical waste. Based on these results and results from the other tests, researchers concluded that distilled water was the best extractant for organic contaminants. The acetate buffer solution simulated the proposed EPA extraction procedure for leaching metals, whereas citrate was considered much more aggressive. In general, the degree of aggressiveness was both medium-dependent and sample-dependent. Also, the leaching method was deemed unsuitable for oily wastes.

Method of contact

The efficiency of an extraction procedure is greatly affected by the means of contact and mixing employed. Kinetic considerations produce quantitative differences between static and mixed contact, as well as between batch and column leaching. The magnitudes of these differences will vary with the waste material being extracted. To date, little work has been performed on the standardization of column tests for chemical wastes. Rather, efforts have been focused on mixed batch extractions employing shakers, mixers, or other means of agitation. One comparative study concluded that while column studies are more realistic, they are more complex and less reproducible because of the potential for channelization of flow in the column. In one series of parallel extractions of chemical wastes, participants in an ASTM survey determined that improper mixing was a major cause of poor reproducibility of results. They concluded that use of a wrist shaker or NBS mixer for 48 h minimized these effect. Similar results were reported by Garrett, *et al* as a result of reviewing a number of studies.

There appears to be general agreement with respect to use of a liquid-to-solid ratio of 10 : 1. While these proportions do not reflect conditions likely to occur in a landfill, they accommodate good mixing and leave ample solution for analysis. Use of room temperature is also generally accepted as appropriate. Landfills may be subjected to a wide range of temperatures, but these are dampened significantly at the bottom of the cells, where the leachate will emerge. If average ground temperature is known, it would be a desirable alternative to room temperature. This degree of sophistication is optional pending the availability of data.

The timing of contact is also an important parameter. As noted previously, participants in the ASTM study believed that 48 h has optimal. Similarly, the state of California originally proposed an approach requiring 48-h contact periods for the first exposure, followed by periods of 4,8, and 16 days. California has subsequently selected a single 48-h contact period. The EPA study, however, concluded that 24 h should be adequate. Their logic was that whereas ideally each solution should be brought to equilibrium, the time required for that endpoint differs between constituents and waste types. Therefore, a long but convenient contact period is optimum. A full 24 h was selected to accommodate scheduling in a laboratory. Certainly, 48 h would also meet those criteria.

The number of leachings is a different question yet. Many proposals to date employ four sequential extractions. These are plotted to determine trends in constant or downward, further work may be deemed unnecessary.

Extract analysis

While it is not the intent of this work to review analytical chemistry or discuss the related technology in depth, it is important to note that differences in round-robin studies of leaching procedures have in part been attributed to differences in analytical results. To provide guidance in this area, the EPA undertook studies to compare EPA, ASTM, and standard methods procedures with respect to variability.

Criteria selection rationales

Once hazards of concern have been selected, specific numeric threshold values or other means of determining when a waste meets a given criteria must be selected. Two approaches to the selection process have been utilized in the past. The first was put forward in the 1973 report to Congress when thresholds were selected to be compatible with values used by other agencies, e.g., U.S. Department of Transportation and U.s. Atomic Energy Commission. The rationale for this approach was to minimize variations indefining hazardous and toxic substances and thereby foster movement to a universal designation. The drawback in this approach is that thresholds designated by other agencies are directed to meeting regulatory needs other than those addressed by hazardous waste management authorities. Therefore, they may be more or less restrictive than necessary, depending on the agency's charter. The appropriateness of thresholds selected strictly for compatibility would therefore be fortuitous.

The second and more recent approach to selection of thresholds is the development of a general risk assessment framework. With this alternative, emphasis is placed on identifying the likely means by which a hazard would be evidenced and selecting thresholds that, under those circumstances, would render that hazard probable. For instance, how toxic must a waste be before it will not be diluted to safe levels in leachate while moving to a potable well? The variations available to this approach and the judgment required in applying them are innumerable.

U.S. environmental protection agency

On May 1980, the EPA published proposed guidelines for defining hazardous wastes. Although numerous tests were considered for possible future use, criteria were established for only four hazards of concern: ignitability, corrosivity, reactivity, and toxicity. The basic rationale behind selection of criteria thresholds was the development of release scenarios to determine what level of properties would pose a hazard under anticipated management practices. Ignitable wastes were defined as liquids with a flash point below 140°F, ignitable compressed gases, oxidizers, and nonliquids that can ignite through spontaneous chemical changes, absorption of moisture, or friction. The flash point of 140 F was chosen over that of 100°F used by DOT to define flammable liquids for regulation of transportation because there is evidence that waste materials are exposed to the higher temperature during handing. Indeed, it has been recommended that the DOT consider modifying its definition to the higher temperature, because ambient temperatures may exceed 100°F in many areas.

The threshold for corrosivity was proposed as materials that corrode SAE 1020 steel at a rate greater than 0.25 inch per year or are aqueous solutions having a pH value greater than or equal to 12 or less than or equal to 3. The former limit was taken directly from corresponding DOT criteria. The latter limits are said to reflect data on skin corrosivity, aquatic toxicity, and heavy-metal solubility.

Reactive wastes are defined by narrative description, with emphasis on ability to detonate, react violently with water, or release toxic fumes when contacted with water. Cyanide- and sulfide-bearing wastes are specifically identified for their potential release of toxic gasses when mixed with dilute acids. Class A and class B explosives are also listed as reactive wastes.

Numerous approaches to selection of toxicity criteria were considered. In the end, it was determined that the major threat posed by improper hazardous waste management lay within contamination of potable water supplies through leachate intrusion. Consequently, toxic wastes were defined as those wastes that, when subjected to a standard leaching test, produced a leachate with constituent concentrations in excess of 100 times the EPA National Interim Primary Drinking WAter Standards. The multiplier of 100 was selected as representative of a conservative level of dilution that may be expected between the point of leaching and potable use from a nearby well. It is based on review of limited data on leachate levels from monitored landfills. The standard leachate test is conducted using distilled water adjusted to pH 5.0 with acetic acid Liquids are filtered or centrifuged from waste after a 24-h agitation period and analyzed for the constituent specified in Table 3-6. additional information on extraction procedures is provided in a subsequent chapter on analytical procedures.

The criteria employed by EPA are meant to test the hazardous nature of any waste. At the same time, the EPA system includes a list of wastes by source or types that have been generically defined as hazardous. The latter is done through a petition. The petition must clearly identify the waste and present result of testing to show that it qualifies for delisting. This process is done on a case-by-case basis. Required tests are those that evaluate the properties for which the waste was originally listed; i.e., if the waste was tested as hazardous because of flammability, the ignitability test should be conducted. The agency currently recommends that generators obtain copies of successful petitions to use as a model.

The process is accelerated if a temporary delisting is requested, rather than a permanent one. Applications for permanent delisting can be submitted after a temporary delisting is granted, so that unnecessary costs are not incurred while awaiting a decision. It was originally thought that the initial surge of delisting activity would be followed by a low-level plateau. Experience has shown that initial registration of wastes was conservative. As costs have increased, more generators are viewing delisting as a means of cutting unnecessary costs. Wastes commonly considered for delisting are plating wastewater treatment sludges and incineration residue.

California

The hazardous waste identification system devised by California blends both pure compound and criteria approaches into a tiered structure. Tiers move from the simpler, inexpensive evaluations to detailed waste stream analysis. Results of the simpler analyses are compared to thresholds with greater safety margins to ensure that the imprecision of the test does not allow hazardous materials to escape the regulatory net.

Individual thresholds were derived from secnario development. For toxicity, six subcategories were incorporated: oral, dermal, inhalation, aquatic, carcinogenic, persistent, and bioaccumulative. A threshold value of LD 5000 mg/kg was selected for oral toxicity in a standard acute rat feeding test. This level was selected by applying a safety factor of 100 to levels deemed to pose a high health hazard by the National Institute for Occupational Safety and Health. In like fashion, california selected a dermal threshold of LD 4300 mg/kg and inhalation thresholds of 10,000 ppm. The threshold for aquatic toxicity was set at LC 500 mg/1. This level was chosen for its compatibility with the limit set by the EPA to select hazardous substances with respect to spills as mandated by Section 311 of the Federal Water pollution Control Act Amendments of 1972.

Criteria for carcinogens were set by a listing/ concentration threshold approach. Wastes are designated as hazardous if they contain a constituent equal to or in excess of 1000 ppm. selected constituents were chosen on the basis of designation as known or suspected carcinogens by the Occupational Safety and Health administration or NIOSH criteria documents. Threshold limits were based on the 1000 ppm minimum level set by OSHA to exempt compositions from workroom regulation as a carcinogen.

Persistent and bioaccumulative materials were similarly dealt with using a listing/ concentration threshold approach. constituents of concern were selected as those materials that persist in the environment and for which man has no major nutritional requirement. Two threshold concentrations are assigned, first, a soluble threshold was established for leachable constituents as 100 times the drinking water or chronic fish toxicity limits. The multiplier of 100 accounts for likely dilution of leachate prior to arrival at a potable well or surface water. This value was based on work performed during development of criteria for the state of Minnesota. The second threshold is a total value set at 100 times the soluble limit for most contaminants. This level was selected arbitrarily as a safety margin.

The flammability criteria were chosen in a manner similar to the proposed EPA criteria. California chose not to seek compatibility with DOT flammable liquid criteria and selected a flash point of <140 F. Explosive and reactive criteria are an expansion on the EPA work incorporating class C as well as class A and B explosives, water-reactive materials, and class 2, 3, and 4 reactive materials as defined by the National Fire Protection Association. Compatibility with existing definitions was also the rationale behind selection of the steel corrosion test. The pH criteria of pH 2 or 12.5 differ from that of the EPA by being less restrictive.

Minnesota

Prior to the adoption of EPA criteria, the Minnesota Pollution Control Agency chose to use a scenarios approach based on landfill disposal of hazardous wastes. Toxicological criteria were specified for oral, dermal, inhalation, aquatic, bioaccumulative, and carcinogenic hazards. The oral threshold of LD_{50} 500 Mg/kg was selected as the toxic amount of the contaminate, assuming that leachate is diluted by a factor of 100 in traveling to a potable well. The dilution factor was selected after a review of empirical leachate data. The dermal threshold of LD_{50} 1000 mg/kg was selected as the toxic level required to be lethal to an operator completely doused with a chemical. The inhalation of LD_{50} 100 mg/ I was selected under the assumption that leachate undergoes the standard 100:1 dilution on traveling through the groundwater and an additional dilution of 100:1 on entering the surface waterbody. Similarly, criteria for specified bioaccumulative agents were selected using the 100:1 and 10,000:1 dilution factors for groundwater and surface water on drinking water and chronic fish limits, respectively.

Corrosive criteria were set at pH 3 and 12 using the same groundwater and surface water dilution factors applied to recommended fish and human exposure limits for acidity and alkalinity, as well as the DOT definition of ability to corrode 0.25 inch or more of SAE 1020 steel in a year. Irritation criteria were selected as materials capable of producing first-or second-degree burns or having a score of 5 or more on the rabbit skin contract evaluation.

Flammable limits differed from DOT standards in that liquids with flash point at or below 200 F were designated as hazardous wastes, as were spontaneously combustible solids. The higher temperature was selected to reflect the contention that during handling, materials will be exposed to temperatures in excess of ambient conditions. Oxidizers and explosive are defined narratively. Minnesota also categorically defined waste oil as hazardous. This last measure reflects the diversity of oils as wastes and the excessive costs that would be associated with bioassay and analysis of oils to determine if they meet criteria.

Washington

The Department of Ecology in Washington took a unique and totally different approach. They built a system from the basic premise that the proposed regulations for Section 311 of the Water Pollution Control Act amendments were directly applicable to hazardous wastes. Interpolating, Washington noted that a harmful quantity would be reached if one had 100 Ib of 1% category A material 100 Ib of 10% equalities and an initial assumption that a material of LD_{50} 50mg/kg is an extremely hazardous waste, the state then extrapolated to designate categories A and B as extremely hazardous, category C as potentially hazardous based on quantity, and category D as dangerous. Designation of complex wastes is made by determining the combined percentage of all constituents in each category and converting to the equivalent total concentration as category A. If this value exceeds 1% and the waste quantity is greater than 100 Ib, the waste is deemed extremely hazardous.

The enabling legislation is Washington also required consideration of persistence and genetic effects. Rather than identify specific compounds, Washington chose to designate all "heavy metals, halogenated hydrocarbons, and aromatic hydrocarbons as persistent and potentially having genetic effects." Wastes are regulated accordingly if they exceed 1% and 100 Ib of these constituents.

Belgium

The definition employed in Belgium is of interest in that it follows the custom of most European countries in taking a listing approach but further modifies this by employing concentration thresholds. This has been a point of controversy when proposed to other members of the commission of the European community. Dissenters have contended as follows.

Concentration is but one factor determining the actual hazard posed by a waste; it should be replaced by a clear definition of the properties of wastes that render them hazardous.

Current knowledges is insufficient to set firm concentration thresholds.

Concentration thresholds do not take into account local conditions that can greatly impact hazard potential.

Concentration thresholds would encourage evasion of rules through partial treatment or dilution.

Be that as it may, Belgium has maintained reliance on concentration levels, as outlined in Article 2 of the law of July 22, 1974, as follows:

> Article 2. The products and by-products which are not used or which cannot be used, the residues and the wastes arising from an industrial, commercial, craft-trade, agricultural or scientific activity shall be regarded as toxic waste:

1. if they are composed principally of one or more of the following chemical substances:
   - (a) the chemical substances distinguished by the symbol, listed at Annex 1 and referred to in Article 723 bis, 4, of the *Reglement general pour la protection de travail*
   - (b) more than 100mg of mercury or of soluble compounds of thallium, expressed as TI ;or
   - (c) more than 500 mg of cadmium or its soluble compounds, expressed as Cd; or
   - (d) more than 250 mg of soluble compounds of beryllium, expressed as Be; or
   - (e) more than 1000 mg of organo-halogen compounds, except polymerized materials and the substances referred to in paragraphs 3,4, and 5;...

3. if they contain pesticides or phytopharamaceutical products enumerated in the lists at Annex II to the Royal Decree of 5 June 1975 on the conservation, commerce and use of pesticides and phytopharamaceuticl products;

4. if they contain more than 10% of organic solvents;

5. if they contain more than 1 mg per kg of dry matter of one or more of the chemical substances enumerated in the lost of carcinogenic substances at Article 148 decies of the general regulation on health and safety at work;

6. if they arise from chemical processes of the pharmaceutical industry, the phytopharamaceutical industry or research laboratories.

Packaging which has contained toxic waste and has been polluted thereby and is not to be reused shall be classed with toxic waste.

Natural ores and worked metals shall not be regarded as toxic waste.

The Belgian concentration levels are applicable throughout the country. The basic criterion is solubility. The toxic wastes are defined by the quantify of chemical substances per kilogram of dry matter.

Criteria in Perspective

Similar rationales and criteria thresholds or modifications thereof have been employed by states and countries other than those presented here to designate hazardous wastes. Further perspective can be gained by noting the relation between criteria selected by various states and the characteristics of common chemicals and fuels as compared in through 3-10 or by reviewing the constituents that have been reported to have been at the source of hazardous waste damage incidents in the past.

As noted previousaly. European nations appear to have taken the course of listing wastes for the purposes of definition. In 1972 the Institution of Chemical Engineers in the United Kingdom published a Provisional Code of Practice for Disposal of Wastes that classified wastes as hazardous and nonhazardous. The former group was further divide into broad groups: flammable, explosive, oxidizing, poisonous, infectious, corrosive, and ratioactive. In Netherlands, proposals for a chemical waste act called for a listing of wastes to be regulated. entative

Prioritizing concern

As is evident from preceding sectarians, even quantitative criteria result in the designation of a wide variety of wastes as hazardous. These wastes may have characteristic properties that span several orders of magnitude. As a consequence, significantly different levels of potential hazard are associated with the overall category of hazardous wastes.

At the same time, there are limited resources available for the management of hazardous wastes. For instance, approved sites for landfill are few in number, and it is becoming increasingly difficult to open new ones. This provides incentive to identify the most hazardous wastes to ensure that they receives the greatest among of attention and the best treatment. Less hazardous wastes should not consume resources needed to properly manage the more toxic or dangerous wastes. Such states as California and Washington have incorporated this philosophy in their enabling legislation by creating a category of extremely hazardous wastes. This provides the regulators with flexibility to specify different levels of management control for wastes posing significantly different hazards by dividing the total waste stream into three categories: extremely hazardous wastes, hazardous or dangerous wastes, and nonhazardous wastes.

Subgrouping in this manner has gained support from several quarters. On reviewing EPA draft regulations, the Manufacturing Chemists Association proposed a system that would control hazardous waste management by adjusting treatment, storage, and disposal standards according to degree of hazard involved. This would provide sufficient flexibility to prevent shortfalls in disposal sites for the extremely hazardous wastes. At the core of the system would be the division of wastes into three categories:

Class 1. highly toxic wastes that are persistent and bioaccumulative and present an extreme hazard to health or to the environment. These wastes require special care in storage, handling, and disposal.

Class II. Wastes that present a moderate hazard and can be handled in a normal manner with standard containers and equipment. These include moderately toxic wastes that are persistent or bioaccumulative and highly toxic wastes that are not persistent or bioaccumulative.

Class III. Wastes that present minimal hazard to health or to he environment when adequately controlled. These include certain corrosive, ignitable, and reactive wastes and those of low or moderate toxicity that are not persistent or bioaccumulative.

Similarly, the Council on Wage and Price Stability submitted a release to the EPA expressing the concerns of the Regulatory Analysis Review Group on the draft RCRA regulations with respect to the need for considering degree of hazard. The final report prepared by the RARG placed major emphasis on the need for a more refined classification system that would include subgroups of hazardous wastes. The RARG's contention was that such a system would provide more protection at lower cost, because the best (and most expensive) sites would be reserved for the costs of handling less hazardous wastes and thus provide less incentive for evasion. it was the RARG's conclusion that use of a single category was an expedient to simplify implementation and enforcement. The net social cost, however, would exceed the associated savings to the agency. As a consequence, the RARG recommended that the EPA pursue the concept of differentiating hazardous wastes by degree of hazard.

Such approaches would segment the waste stream into discrete packages with associated levels of priority. Priority can also established on a continuum. an approach to this was first offered in the 1973 report to Congress. Wastes were compared on the basis of a ranking factor defined as $R = Q/CP$

where R is ranking factor, Q is annual production quantity for a waste, and *CP* is the critical product for the waste being considered. The critical product was further defined as the product of the lowest environmental concentration at which a waste would manifest any hazard of concern and an index representing the waste's mobility in the environment. Hence, a waste that is miscible in water or highly volatile would be considered more of a hazard than a relatively immobile waste.

The prioritization formulation is simple, but it requires further development to create a consistent from for the mobility index. Once a proper dimensionless index has been selected, the resulting ranking factor has units of volume per year representative of the volume of environment potentially contaminated to a hazardous level. Klee pointed out than the flaws of this approach is that by relying on the smallest concentration at which a hazard is evidenced, all remaining data on other hazard types are ignored. This constitutes a tacit assumption that all hazards are of equal concern. When comparing between wastes, the ranking fails to recognize that even though two materials may have similar critical concentrations, one poses greater additional hazards at slightly higher critical concentrations.

This defect is also shared in part by the model developed by Pavoni, Hagerty, and Lee . In this methodology, criteria were established in five areas:

1. Human toxicity = 12 x Sax rating
2. Groundwater toxicity = 6 (4—log of the smallest critical concentration)
3. Disease transmission potential = index assigned on scale of 0 to 105

4. Biological persistence = 16 (1-BOD/TOD), where BOD is biochemical oxygen demand, and TOD is theoretical oxygen demand
5. Mobility = 7-*C* + log solubility, where *C* is net charge of waste determined form molecular formula in reaction with water pH 7

The hazard ranking itself is calculated as the sum of these criteria. Some of the hazardous data not covered by the smallest critical concentration value are recoupled through the additional factors; so this model is more comprehensive in scope than the previous one. No rationale is give for the selection of weighting factors incorporated in the summing process.

Some of the intent of the MCA proposal for waste grouping, as well as prioritization of individual wastes, is encompassed in e system employed by the Texas Water Quality Board for classifying industrial wastes with respect to possible impacts from improper land disposal. The three categories are defined as follows.

Class III. Essentially inert and essentially insoluble industrial solid waste, usually including materials such as rock, brick, glass, dirt, certain plastics, rubber etc., that are not readily decomposable

Class II. Organic and inorganic industrial solid waste that is readily decomposable in nature and contains no hazardous waste materials.

Class I. All waste materials not classified as class II or III, normally including all industrial solid waste in liquid from and all hazardous wastes

The subgrouping here segments the nonhazardous wastes, however, rather than the hazardous wastes. The latter category is subsequently dealt with through a proportization ranking.

In an analysis of potential RCRA site failures and their effect of fund balance in the PCLTF, Battelle devised a simplified scheme for ranking hazardous waste constituents by hazard. The rating *R* was derived as

$$R= [\log (S/cc) -\log (Kd)]$$

where S-solubility of the constituent, cc = critical concentration of the constituent, either detection limit or toxic threshold depending on the triggering event of interest, and Kd = distribution constant for the constiotuent between soil and water.

The rating was based on breaches of contaminant and subsequent contamination of drinking water supplies. As a consequence, the *cc* value refer to human health concerns. In essence, the rating prioritizes constituents by mobility, that is, the earliest that arrives at a toxic concentration receives the highest rating.

Categorization of wastes is also being contemplated as and outcome of landfill ban regulations. Groups such as EPA and the state of California are evaluating criteria to identify those waste that will be banned from land disposal. This constituents a degree of hazard concept for a subset of waste disposal options.

Numerous other approaches to proportization can be and have been devised. All have several elements in common. The first is the selection of hazards of concern to be considered. The second is the mechanism by which exposure probability is evaluated. The third is the selection of a weighting system for integrating inputs on the various hazards. In all three areas there is opportunity for employing arbitrary index valued or quantitative data. Subjective judgment enters in and thereby creates a bias or prejudice in the ranking based on the orientation of the developer. Hence, even when two systems are devised to use the same input data, they may result in significantly different rankings. Klee has suggested that this may be avoided by use on an additive utility model that provides and explicit and logically consistent a part of the hazardous waste regulation development process. However, the rapidly developing area of chemical risk assessment appears to offer an attractive framework for equitable prioritization.

European approaches to categorization of wastes reflect their heavy commitment of listing approaches. For instance, Article L231-6 of the French labor law established five categories of waste: (1) chemical compound groups, as well as a list of some 200 specific chemicals, (2) radioactive contaminated materials, and selected industry-specific wastes.

Similarly, wastes in the Netherlands are grouped as follows:

Class A : Mercury and cadmium compounds, oil

compounds of comparable damage potential; includes toxic, bioaccumulative, and persistent materials present at levels greater 50 mg/kg.

Class B1: Heavy-metal compounds whose toxicity occurs at levels greater than those for class A; chemical wastes when concentration exceeds 5000mg/kg, as well as organic compounds whose extraction, manufacture, or synthesis is industry-related, other than polymers.

Class B II: Elements or compounds that release acute, volatile toxic materials when contacted with water.

Class C: Inorganic compounds present at levels in excess of 20,000 mg/kg, and some organic compounds similar to those in class BI.

Class D: Reactive elements and compounds that are not toxicologically harmful, and inorganic with corrosive properties at concentrations greater than 50,000 mg/kg.

An issue related to prioritization of hazardous wastes is the determination of minimum exemption quantities. The initial EPA draft regulations and some states have implied that small quantities of hazardous wastes are of sufficiently low priority that they can be exempted from regulation. Exemption quantities have been defined as anywhere from 1 Ib of category A waste to 100kg per month. In the latter case, ad distinction is made for extremely hazardous wastes, where the exemption quantity is reduced to 1 kg. Prior to 1980, the EPA proposed no distinction. As a result, a generator would have been exempted if he produced 990 kg/month of dioxin, one of the most toxic chemicals known to man. The Regulatory Analysis Review Group took EPA to task on this proposal. They concluded that small- quantity exemptions are justified only when tied to consideration of the degree of hazard involved, in a fashion similar to the categorization scheme used by Washington. Once again, at the core of the question is the trade-off between the economic impact of complying with regulations and the net social benefit of regulating small quantities of waste. The case for tying exemption quantities to degrees of hazard is underscored, because the net social benefit goes up with the intrinsic hazard of the waste.

Similar considerations have also given rise to the declaration of special wastes. Because of large volumes and the massive potential economic impact, regulatory authorities have taken to exempting certain extremely high volume wastes that might otherwise be designated hazardous. Creation of these special categories allows less restrictive and less costly disposal practices to be used. The proposed RCRA regulations have specified three types of wastes for exemptions: (1) sludges from publicly owned treatment plants, (2) agricultural crop residues and manures intended for spreading back on the land, and (3) mining overburden and tailings scheduled for return to the mine site. In addition, the following wastes have been classified as special wastes subject to a different set of standards: (1) cement kiln dust, (2) utility waste (flash, bottom ash, and scrubber sludge), (3) mining wastes, and (4) gas and oil drilling muds and oil production brines.

3 The Regulation of Hazardous Waste Management

Historical perspective

For the most part, hazardous wastes are a relatively new segment of the total solid waste stream. Whereas solid wastes can be traced back to the middens in the camps of primitive man at the dawn of human emergence, hazardous wastes are largely a product of the industrial age, when man first began to utilize fossil fuels and synthesize chemical entities. Thus it is that D.G. Wilson's delightful history of solid waste management begins with Moses' instruction to bury wastes as a means of disposal, and it traces developments through Crete, Rome, England, Medieval Europe, and colonial America; but no mention is made of materials that would be defined as hazardous wastes until subsequent sections devoted to the discussion of industrial waste management. The excerpts from publications and official documents focus on the odor and nuisance problems associated with rubbish. In a review of tort and statutory law concerning environmental issues, Krier provided a glimpse of the awakening to the fact that wastes may pose a specific hazard. Although it was litigated under common nuisance law, the case of Versailles Brough v. McKeesport Coal and Coke Company dealt with specific hazards associated with gob piles from coal mining Gob is the solid interlayed coal and shale material wasted during early coal mining because of its low fuel value. It became a nuisance because it often spontaneously ignited and would burn for great periods of time. Because many types of solid, nonhazardous refuse are also spontaneously ignitable, it is doubtful to what extent the gob would meet modern hazard criteria based on flammability. However, gob would meet modern hazard criteria based on flammability. However, gob releases sulfur dioxide when burned and therefore generates toxic off-gases. In the more recent case of Warehak v. Moffat suit, was brought as a result of toxic hydrogen sulfide emissions from culm banks that destroyed the paint on a nearby house. Similarly, Oregon has been the site of two related cases involving negligence and strict liability and nuisance and trespass as a result of waste discharges bearing fluorine, hydrogen and calcium fluoride, and silicon tetrafluoride causing health and property damage. Aside from the precedence of the legal points made during the litigation, these often-cited cases illustrate the shift from the nuisance and odor problems of solid wastes referenced by Wilson to those of toxic hazards arising from industrial wastes. Contemporary legislation and regulation in the United States reflect the same shift in emphasis as it was developed in response to the evolving recognition of waste-related problems.

Wilson related the first known U.S. ordinance in refuse as one adopted by the Corporation of Georgetown in 1795 prohibiting the extended storage of refuse on private property and the dumping of refuse in the street. Soon after, carters were brought under contract to periodically remove refuse from streets and alleys. Solid waste management remained largely a local issue throughout the next century. The major solid waste problems arose in the large cities, where dense population combined with lack of available land for disposal to create a high-demand/low-supply situation. Ordinances and systems for management varied widely between metropolitan areas. Federal action first emerged in 1899 with the Rivers and Harbors Act, which prohibited the disposal of solid objects in waterways such that they would create a hazard to navigation. Although this would appear very indirect, it formed the basis for the limited degree of solid waste management regulations over the next 50 yr. It became known as the "Refuse Act" and provided the legal foundation for Crops of Engineers discharge permits, the forerunner of NPDES permits.

The first major piece of legislation directed specifically to solid waste management was the Solid Waste Disposal Act of 1965. This act continued the philosophy that solid waste management was basically a local or state problem, but it recognized that a national effort was required to coordinate a program that could transcend the technical and economic capabilities of local communities. To facilitate improvements in local and state programs, the act authorized specific actions in six areas:

1. Grants to demonstrate new and improved waste disposal technology on local and state levels
2. Grants to foster regional solid waste management systems in areas fragmented into small communities
3. Grants for conduct of statewide solid waste management need surveys and subsequent state plan development
4. Funds for direct research and grants to develop new approaches to solid waste management
5. Funds for direct support and grants focused on creating training programs
6. Technical assistance to local and state entities with solid waste management problems.

In this way, PL 89-272 established several key tenets for the federal role in solid waste management. The most obvious is maintenance of the local entity as the functional organization in the management system. Although the need for regional management plans is clearly narrated, Congress intentionally left this to the local decision makers narrated, congress intentionally left this to the local decision makers rather than create federal boundaries, as had been done for Air Quality Regions. The character of federal involvement was defined as that embodied in economic support and technology transfer. The administration would act as a resource pool to be drawn on at local discretion. No federal standards were set to create uniformity. Similarly, no formal recognition of a hazardous waste management problem was evident.

Continually mounting concern over protection of the environment led to a second legislative measure, the Resource Recovery Act of 1970. Although the title reflects a swing in solid waste management philosophy from the disposal language of the 1965 act, the Resource Recovery Act took the form of a series of amendments to the earlier act. The heavy reliance on state and local control of solid waste management was kept intact, but new sections were added to expand the scope of federal involvement. Specific additions included:

1. The statement of purpose for the act was expanded to cover provision for promulgation of guidelines for solid waste management.
2. Research and grant activity was revised to encourage heavy emphasis on waste reduction and resource recovery, with a special study and demonstration projects mandated on recovery of useful energy and materials.
3. The secretary was directed to provide recommended guidelines for all phases of solid waste management, as well as model codes, ordinances and statutes for implementation of those guidelines.

4. All executive agencies and their contractors were directed to ensure compliance with guidelines promulgated under the act.
5. The secretary was mandated to provide a comprehensive report and plan for creation of a system of national disposal sites for the storage and disposal of hazardous wastes.

The final amendment, that calling for a study of a national hazardous waste disposal system, offers two important features: (1) a recognition that some solid waste management problems cannot be handled at the local level and (2) the first direct mention of hazardous waste management in federal legislation. These changes are embodied in Section 212 of the amended solid Waste Disposal Act, which has been reprinted in the previous chapter. The results of the subsequent report to Congress were to become the forerunner of current hazardous waste law. In authorizing the study and plan, Congress was expressing three discrete concerns:

1. Hazardous materials and wastes, regardless of origin, represented a substantial and growing threat to public health and environmental quality.
2. Management of such wastes was inadequate, and the need for responsible stewardship would increase in the future.
3. The problems posed in the management of hazardous wastes did not necessarily recognize state boundaries, and the materials in

> question were derived from a variety of sources, both private an public, therefore, consideration had to be given to the feasibility of establishing a national system of disposal sites.

As a consequence, the report to Congress was undertaken in the spirit of defining a new national goal: In order to protect the public health and welfare and the quality of the environment, present practices in disposal of hazardous waste materials must be significantly improved, and a framework for responsible stewardship established.

The report was prepared by the then newly formed Environmental Protection Agency, drawing on the inputs of six private contractors. It was presented to Congress of June 30, 1973. The report concluded the following: (1) A significant hazardous waste management problem did in fact exist and was growing steadily; (2) technological solutions for the problem were available, for the most part, but represented a significant increase in processing costs; (3) the legislative and economic adequate disposal practices in most instances; (4) the cost-effective solution appeared to be a program centered around regulation of hazardous waste treatment/disposal; (5) a small but viable hazardous waste management industry existed and could expand if a regulatory program created a larger market; however, economic and other uncertainties precluded accurate assessment of the private sector's response; (6) alternatives were available for governmental involvement in providing services, but the necessity of such a course of action was in doubt.

The report to Congress clearly amplified the new directions resulting from section 212 of the amended Solid Waste Disposal Act: identification of the hazardous waste management subset of overall solid waste management, and the need for a federal role in subsequent programs. Pursuant to the latter point, the EPA appended to the report a draft of the proposed Hazardous Waste Management Act of 1973. The EPa was not without support for such a move. In the previous month, the National Association of Counties Research Foundation had concluded that the dimensions and complexities of the hazardous waste management problem set were such that regulation and enforcement of standards should be at a national level. In fact, the foundation suggested that local involvement should be minimized, save for th authority to impose stricter standards on a local-option basis.

This set the stage for major federal legislation on the management of hazardous wastes. In anticipation, the Environmental protection Agency identified funding and initiated an ambitious program to provide a more quantitative focus on waste generation and the status of management practices. As data were collected, they were passed on the congressional staffers to provide impetus for passage of the desired legislation. Concomitant pressures for toxic substance control legislation and comprehensive solid waste management legislation muddied the issue and helped delay action for several years. In the end, the architects of environmental legislation within the government chose to maintain the close ties between hazardous wastes and solid wastes. The proposed hazardous Waste Management Act of 1973 became but one element, albeit an important one, of proposed comprehensive legislation for solid waste management. This took its final form as Subtitle C of the Resource Conservation and Recovery Act of 1976, which replaced the amended Solid Waste Disposal act in its entirety.

RCRA

The Resource Conservation and Recovery Act constitutes a clear and unmistakable shift to federal standards and regulations for solid waste management, with enforcement at the state level when implementation plans are deemed acceptable. The heavy federal role is particularly evident in Subtitle C: Hazardous Waste Management. Subtitle C is divided into 11 major sections prescribing a complete regulatory control program. Each section is summarized below.

3001. Identification and listing of hazardous wastes

The administration is required to promulgate criteria that identify the characteristics of hazardous wastes and allow the listing of those wastes. At the same time, regulations are to be issued that identify hazardous Wastes.

The administration is required to promulgate criteria that identify the characteristics of hazardous wastes and allow the listing of those wastes. At the same time, regulations are to be issued that identify hazardous waste characteristics and list specific hasardous wastes. Fulfillment of these mandates creates a working definition of hazardous wastes that can be applied to any candidate waste for classification. State governors are afforded the option of petitioning for classification or listing of a specific material as a hazardous waste. Section 3001 defines the breadth of the law's coverage, because it determines which materials will be defined as hazardous.

3002. Standards applicable to generators of hazardous wastes

The administrator is required to promulgators respecting:

Recordkeeping practices relating to production, composition, and disposition of hazardous wastes

Labeling of containers used for storage, transport, or disposal

Use of appropriate containers

Providing information on the composition of wastes to parties transporting, treating, strong, or disposing of wastes

Use of a manifest system to provide for tracking of wastes throughout the management cycle, save those wastes disposed on site

Generating periodic reports on hazardous waste activities

Section 3002 delineates the responsibilities of the waste generator and, in so doing, establishes sufficient data on the sources of hazardous wastes to accommodate cradle-to-gave management.

3003. Standards applicable to transporters of hazardous wastes

The administrator is to promulgate regulations establishing standards for the transporters of hazardous wastes that will include:

Requirements for recordkeeping concerning wastes shipped

Prohibitions on transport of improperly labeled wastes

Operational mode for compliance with the prescribed manifest system requirement to deliver wastes only to permitted facilities designated on the manifest form

The administrator is required to coordinate the foregoing regulations with the secretary of transportation in those cases where hazardous wastes are deemed to be subject to the Hazardous Materials Transportation Act. Section 3003 provides the important information link to connect the tracking system between point of origin and final resting place.

3004. Standards applicable to owners and operators of hazardous waste treatment, storage, and disposal facilities

The administrator is required to promulgate standards and regulations for facilities that treat, store, and dispose of hazardous wastes. Regulatory control is prescribed for:

Maintenance of records on the quantities, nature, and disposition of all hazardous wastes received.

Reporting, monitoring, and inspection of manifests for wastes received to assure compliance.

Management of wastes in a manner acceptable to the administrator Location, design, and construction of facilities

Contingency plans for action to minimize unanticipated damage

Operation of facilities, including such aspects as ownership qualification, continuity of operation, training, and financial responsibility Compliance with permit requirements

Section 3004 constitutes the regulatory framework for treatment and disposal of hazardous wastes, thus complementing the controls placed on generation and transport in previous sections. In many respects, it is the heart of the issue raised by the report to Congress. Other sections merely provide the mechanisms and data that will facilitate implementation and enforcement of Section 3004 regulations.

3005. Permits for treatment, storage, and disposal of hazardous wastes

The administrator is required to establish a permit system such that all parties engaged in treatment, storage, or disposal must obtain permits in order to continue in those activities. Permits will define the extent and nature of those activities. The permit application will include a projection of waste loads, types and frequencies anticipated, and a description of the site. Permit status until such time as the agency has officially processed an application thereto. Section 3005 established the means by which the agency can enforce the 3004 regulations, namely through certification with a permit process. To date, most facilities have been granted interim status awaiting development of guidelines and procedures to support a full-fledged permit program. By late 1984. EPA and other authorized states began to call in applications for part B permits, but only five land disposal facilities were fully permitted. it was estimated at that time that it would take 10 years to process permits for the 2000 sites likely to apply.

3006. Authorized state hazardous waste programs

The administrator is required to promulgate guidelines to assist states in the development of state hazardous waste programs. States wishing to administer and enforce the hazardous waste regulatory program can be authorized to do so if this application is accepted on the grounds that (1) the state program is equivalent (criteria for equivalence will be defined by the agency) to the federal program, (2) The state program is not inconsistent with the federal or other state programs, and (3) the enforcement of the program is adequate to promote compliance. Interim authorization is granted to states with existing programs that are substantially equivalent to the federal program. Authorized state programs, when enforced, will carry the same force and effect as the federal program. Should enforcement be found inadequate, authorization can be revoked.

Section 3006 provides the mechanism by which the federal program can be brought back to the state level for enforcement, much as has been done with air quality regulation.

3007 Inspections

The administrator or his designated representative is provided the right to gain entry to facilities and records where hazardous wastes are generated, treated, stored, or disposed for the purpose of inspection and sampling. Records, reports, and information resulting from inspections are available to the public, unless the operator can demonstrate to the administrator's satisfaction that release would divulge information privileged to protection. Section 3007 provides one means of monitoring regulatory compliance.

The framework of Subtitle C is such that it places total reliance on private industry to met the needs for hazardous waste management. No provisions have been made for federal activities beyond the regulatory role. Hence, the loans and loan guarantees alluded to in the 1973 report to Congress did not survive the legislation process. On the other hand, the act does not preclude local and state governments from undertaking some aspects of hazardous waste management such as private industry might. Such action would be subject to the same degree of regulation and would, for all intents and purposes, parallel facets of solid waste management where municipal collection systems operate in direct competition with private services.

As with many environmental laws. The extent and nature of RCRA's impact will be closely tied to the content of regulations promulgated as a result of the act. The effectiveness of the resulting management program and indirect effects on commerce will be determined by such features as 91) the rationale employed for selecting criteria to define hasardous wastes, 92) the criteria themselves, 93) the use of performance versus design standards, (4) the standards selected for acceptance of permit applications, and (5) the scope of financial responsibility requirements.

While Subtitle C is relatively comprehensive, it leaves some unanswered questions. The issue of federal financial assistance or incentives to sponsor private activities has been discussed. The law also fails to address the problem of abandoned or closed disposal sites that may be causing environmental problems. The "imminent hazard" provisions of Section 7003 gives the administrator a means of restraining operators whose activities present an imminent and substantial endangerment to health or the environment, but they do not include funds or mechanisms for remedial action to stop leachate, vapor loss, or other natural mechanisms that will continue to spread contaminants after cessation of operations. Hence, the law is directed to prevention of future Love Canal incidents, but offers no remedy for those sites whose origins predate promulgation of new regulations or for sites operated outside of the law.

RCRA does not provide the EPA or the Justice Department with the power of subpoena. This may severely cripple efforts to enforce subsequent regulations. The development of hazardous waste legislation and regulations has been continually hampered by lack of data on the current situation.

As the prospects of litigation and major penalties become increasingly likely, data will become even more difficult to obtain. implementation will also be weekended by the lack of adequate funds for the development of state programs. Because the EPA is not properly staffed to administer RCRA in all the states, successful implementation will depend on certification of state programs. However, the $50 million allocated for development of the necessary programs appear considerably short of the actual requirements. This has put increased emphasis on the evaluation of fee systems such as those imposed in maryland and California.

CERCLA

Whereas RCRA was deemed necessary, in part, because evidence was found of significant damages resulting from improper disposal of chemical wastes, it is ironic that RCRA include no sections addressing the "sins of the past." With the discovery of sites such as Love Canal and the Valley of Drums, the oversight became evident. Public pressure mounted until Congress constructed and passed the Comprehensive Environmental Response, Compensation and Liability Act of 1980. PL 96-510. To a great extent, CERCLA addresses some of the financial responsibility aspects of hazardous waste management. In particular, CERCLA establishes two funds to aid in compensation for damages arising from hazardous-waste-related incidents; (i) Superfund and (2) the Post-Closure Liability Trust Fund (PCLTF).

Superfund. Superfund is the central feature of CERCLA. For many people it was the major reason for passage of the act...essence, Superfund is a pool of money generated by special taxes to ensure that funds are available to pay for removal or remedial action in response to release of hazardous materials. It can be likened to the National Contingency Fund for response to release of hazardous materials. It can be likened to the National Contingency Fund for response to hazardous materials. It can be likened to the National Contingency Fund for response to hazardous material spills, with a broader charter for the types of situations that are covered. In the case of Superfund, monies are collected from a tax of $0.79 per barrel of crude oil received at U.S. refineries or per barrel of petroleum products refined outside the country and received for use. In addition, a schedule of specified tax rates is established for 42 other chemical substances. These taxes constitute 87.5% of the fund monies. The remainder comes from the U.S. Treasury. Fund outlays may include payment for damages to natural resources, limited studies of resource damage, resource restoration, enforcement and abatement actions against releases, epidemiology, response cost and safety, as well as the prescribed remedial action. The fund cannot be used to cover personal injuries. This remains a controversial issue, with critics claiming that failure to consider injuries constitutes a judgment "that property is more significant than human beings". The fund itself guarantees the availability of monies to perform the foregoing actions. if parties can be identified that are responsible for the damages, the fund can seek compensation and replenish itself. In the case of unknown parties or an inability to bear the financial burden, the fund is diminished accordingly.

Superfund was passed on the basis of a large number of known or suspected sites where hazardous wastes were improperly disposed. However, provisions were included to cover sites identified or created in the future and to mandate reporting of said sites. Section 103 of the act requires that, unless exempted, any person who owned or operated a site at which hazardous substances were stored, treated, or disposed must notify the EPA. Notification was required by June 9, 1981. Compliance generated a list of candidate sites for remedial action that has subsequently been reviewed for prioritization. In addition, the act requires that release of quantities exceeding 1 Ib or an otherwise specified reportable quantity must be reported immediately to the EPA if not allowed under existing federal permits. Hence, spills not covered by Section 311 of the water Pollution control Act Amendments of 1972 (WPCA) are now reportable and can be responded to using federal founds. Substances requiring spill notification include those designated as hazardous under the clear water, clean air, and RCRA laws, toxic pollutants as identified under Section 307 (a) of FWPCA, and imminently hazardous chemical substances or mixtures subject to action under Section 7 of the Toxic substances Control Act.

PCLTF. The Post-Closure Liability Trust Fund (PCLTF) is the least publicized of the two CERCLA funds. It was established to provide for remedial action and damages arising from chemical contamination associated with sites operated and closed in compliance with RCRA. As currently structured, the EPA will qualify sites for coverage under the PCLTF. Criteria will include operation and closure with a RCRA permit, and observations for up to five years that there is no substantial likelihood of significant risk. Upon qualification, the federal government takes responsibility for all post-closure cases after a period of up to 30 years, as well as all claims arising from chemical losses. The latter can include damages to natural resources up to $50 million, continued monitoring and maintenance, remedial action, and compensation for injuries or loss. Hence, unlike Superfund, the PCLTF addresses injury and personal claims arising from chemical migration.

The fund is created by a tax of $2-13 per dry ton of hazardous waste disposed at a facility. Collection begins on September 30, 1983, and continues until the fund reaches $200 million. The tax is then suspended until such time as the fund drops below the #200 million level. Additional revenues to the fund include interest and other income related to fund management. Hence, if claims are low, the fund could sustain itself without the tax, after initially reaching the $200 million threshold. On the other hand, if claims are high, the threshold may be inadequate and taxes may have to be increased. Recognizing that the tax rate and the threshold were selected arbitrarily, Congress mandated a study of the likelihood of claims so that readjustments could be considered.

The finding of that study indicate the fund will be inadequate within the first 50 yr of its existence. Since all landfills will eventually leak in some manner, migration of contaminants will occur and ultimately put demands on the fund. These demands will mount until funds are exhausted. This finding has led to increased scrutiny of landfill bans for selected wastes and serious reconsideration of the efficacy of the PCLTF. At the same time, the Department of Treasury concluded that no private insurance programs were available to replace the PCLTF. and that such programs were not likely without well-defined limits on liability. Hence, if the PCLTF is not activated, long-term liability concerns may significantly increase the estimate life-cycle costs of landfills for hazardous wastes.

NCP. Section 105 of CERCLA requires the EPA to issue a revised National Contingency Plan to reflect the emergency response and remedial action requirements arising from the act, as well as the traditional needs arising out of Section 311 of the WPCA. This proved to be a major point of controversy. The EPA had great difficult in deciding upon a tone and level of detail for the CEP. As a consequence, promulgation was delayed until JUly 16, 1982. In the interim, state and environmental organizations threatened suites of mandamus and other action to force promulgation. The NCP became a linchpin for all of Superfund, because remedial action was to be in compliance with the NCP. With promulgation, Superfund activity enjoyed rapid growth, even though controversy arose over the content of the NCP. A brief synopsis of that content pertaining to hazardous wastes in provided next.

Subpart B: Responsibility. The duties of the president as specified in CERCLA are delegated to the EA and U.S. Coast Guard with a mandate to coordinate with state and local authorities. Other federal agencies are required to make resources of facilities available for assistance when appropriate. Responsibilities include those to include those to coordinate and direct all public and private efforts to abate the threat. Some federal agencies have duties established by statute. All agencies must report releases covered by CERCLA. In addition:

The Department of Health Services is delegated authorities for health-related work, e.g., hazard assessments and surveys.

The Federal Emergency Management Agency is delegated authorities with respect to permanent relocation of residents.

The Department of Defense is delegated all authorities to implement CERCLA for release of DOD properties/facilities.

States are encouraged to assign offices to participate in the process and to address situations not eligible for federal funding. Participation by non-government groups is encouraged.

Subpart C: Organization. National planning and coordination is conducted by the National Response Team, a committee of representatives from affected agencies, with the EPA representatives servings as chairman. The NRT is also the central point for all communications about response activities. Regional planning and preparedness actions prior to a response RRT has a similar structure as the NRT, using regionally assigned agency staff. The On-Scene Commander is responsibly for developing local contingency plans as well as for direction of all emergency response activities. The National Strike Force consists of USCG strike teams available to support the OSC upon request. The Emergency Response TEam consists of EPA personnel or delegates trained to evaluate, monitor, and supervise response as well as proved ,limited "initial aid" actions. Scientific support for response is provided by the Scientific Support Coordinator. Public information activities are conducted by the USCG Public Information Assist Team (PIAT) and the EPA Public Affairs Assist Team (PAAT).

SubpartD: Plans. Regional and, where practicable, local contingency plans are required.

Subpart F: Hazardous Substance Response. CERCLA is to be employed for removal or remedial action when it is deemed necessary because other responsible parties cannot or will not take proper action. Fund conservation dictates that attempts be made to encourage state or industrial action where possible. Discovery may result from Section 103 or 104 required action or other activities and must be followed by prompt notification of the cognizant OSC. At that time, the lead agency must make a preliminary assessment of the scope of the problem. If imminent hazard is determined, immediate removal action to a ceiling of $1 million is to be is to be initiated, but should not exceed 6 months time to complete. The NCP provides a general list of actions that can be taken as a part of immediate removal. As soon as practicable, an evaluation is made to determine if further response is required through planned removal and remedial action. Studies can be authorized as required to support the evaluation. States may submit sites for priority ranking and designate the highest priority within the state. These will be collated into a national priority list, which, if practicable, will always have the top priority from each state in the top 100 sites. Planned removal may be conducted under federal direction and contracting, or if a cooperative agreement is signed, the state may take the lead role. In either event, planned removal must be requested by the governor, along with assurances that the state will cover 10% all costs of the action, or at least 50% or greater, as determined by EPA, depending on the degree of responsibility borne by the state or political subdivision thereof. If continued action is not required immediately to prevent and emergency, planned removals should not exceed $1 million or 6 months. Guidelines are provided for determining when a planned removal is warranted. Remedial actions are those directed to effecting a permanent solution. Once again, guidelines ar provided to help is to be prepared, with each entry undergoing screening with respect to costs, effects, and feasibility. A detailed analysis is conducted on those alternatives that emerge well from the screening process. Documentation is maintained throughout the process to support any cost-recovery action. A list is provided of methods for remedying releases.

Subpart G: Trustees for natural Resources.. Responsible federal agencies are designated as trustees for specific resources that may be damaged by a release. States may also act as trustees. In either case, trustees are responsible for assessing natural resource losses, seeking recovery for those losses, and devising and implementing plans for restoration, rehabilitation, and replacement.

Other Features of CERCLA. Other features of importance in CERCLA include the designation of an assistant administration of EPA for solid wastes. This marks the first time that an individual in the agency has been charged with the responsibility for solid wastes and given authority on a par with AA's for water, air, and toxic substances. In some respects, this signals the final" coming of age"for solid waste in balancing concern for the physical environment.

CERCLA also contains requirements for a number of studies. These include the following:

Post-Closure Insurance: (a) A a Treasury Department study of the feasibility of establishing an optimum system of private insurance for post-closure. (b) A presidential study of whether or not adequate private insurance coverage is available for liability claims. (c) An EPA study of the need for a adequate tax revenue for the PCLTF.

Hazardous Waste Facilities: An EPA report to Congress on issues, alternatives, and policy related to the selection of optimum location for hazardous waste facilities.

Industry Taxes: A joint EPA/Treasury study of potential additions to the hazardous waste lists and appropriate tax rates to support the PCLTF.

Employee Protection: An EPA study evaluating the potential loss of employment from administration and enforcement of CERCLA.

Worker Safety: A joint EPA/OSHA/NIOSH study to modify the NCP as necessary.

Natural Resources: A presidential study of losses to natural resources caused by losses of oil and hazardous substances.

Legal Redress: A 12-member panel of lawyers is required to study the adequacy of existing common law and statutory remedies to provide legal redress for harm to man and the environment from releases.

Superfund Implementation: A presidential report to Congress on how successfully Superfund is being implemented.

Use of Superfund Cleanup Authorities: A joint EPA/ attorney-general study to establish guidelines for using imminent hazard, enforcement, and emergency response authorities.

While CERCLA itself speaks to issues not addressed in RCRA, there are obvious areas of interface. Clearly, the previously listed studies on pst-closure insurance relate to financial responsibility elements of RCRA regulations. The study of a hazardous waste facility's siting is directly responsive to RCRA concerns while that on industry taxes may lead to chages in Section 3001. Similarly, CERCLA specifies use of RCRA definition of hazardous waste when determining which wastes are subject to the PCLTF tax. On the other side, RCRA regulations have been formulated to reflect CERCLA. For instance, before RCRA permits will be approved for existing facilities, existing contaminant plumes must be removed and/ or mitigated. Other areas of implied interface have not been developed. As previously noted, the revised NCP is strangely silent on the need for remedial actions to be performed in accordance with RCRA requirements.

Growing dissatisfaction in Congress with the way EPA has chosen to promulgate hazardous waste management programs, and insights gained in retrospect have raised several issues of concern. These have subsequently formed the basis for proposal amendments and reauthorization bills for CERCLA.

As is evident from the 1984 RCRA amendments, Congress has chosen to move much more deeply into he specifics of regulatory programs rather than create a broad legislative net from which EPA can define a program. This clearly illustrates a growing conflict between the legislative and administrative branches with respect to implementation of environmental programs and has been evidenced in debates over other pending CERCLA amendments.

Key issues discussed in the debate over reauthorization of CERCLA have included broader topics such as the need to increase the size of Superfund tenfold and the need for victim compensation mechanisms. Both topics are extremely controversial and have raised real possibilities of a a presidential veto.

Federal Water Pollution Control Acts

These acts contain several sections dealing specifically with toxic effluents and hazardous substances from the standpoint of acute and chronic discharges. If a hazardous waste includes a designated material, its direct discharge to navigable waters could constitute violation of regulations under either of these sections.

Through Sections 301 and 304, effluent limitations and guidelines are established for direct discharge. Sections 307b and 307c complement these with pretreatment standards for wastes destined for public sewage treatment facilities. Sections 403 and 404 address guidelines for ocean discharge and disposal of dredge and fill materials. The latter lines for ocean discharge and disposal of dredge and fill materials. The latter may include materials qualifying as hazardous wastes. In addition to these direct impacts on hazardous waste management, the federal water pollution control acts influence hazardous waste management by creating treatment requirements that will result in sludges qualifying as hazardous wastes. Hence, the residuals burden is shifted further from water to land.

Marine Protection, Research, And Sanctuaries Act, Pl 92-532

The act establishes regulatory control over the dumping of materials into the ocean. This and the federal water pollution control acts and the Rivers and Harbors Act of 1899 combine to form a relatively comprehensive package eliminating the use of ocean disposal for management of hazardous wastes.

Safe Drinking Water Act, Pl 93-523

While this act focuses largely on the development of primary and secondary standards for drinking water quality, the need to protect underground sources of water has given rise to a mandate for development of an underground injection control program. As currently interpreted, this constitutes the regulation of deep-well injection facilities. Currently, coverage is not extended to pits, ponds, or lagoons that may threaten potable aquifers through percolation. That aspect of waste management is left to RCRA.

Federal Insecticide, Fungicide, and Rodenticide Act Pl 92-516

Section 19a of this act requires the EPA to establish regulations for the storage and disposal of pesticide containers, excess pesticides, and pesticides for which registration has been canceled. Because many of these materials are likely to be defined as hazardous waste, resultant regulations relate directly to those required by Section 3004 of RCRA. Similarly, Section 16 regulations on labeling will interface with labeling requirements in Section 3002 an 3003 of RCRA.

Toxic substances Control Act, Pl 94-469

the Toxic Substances Control Act was enacted as a means of regulating the entry of toxic substances in to society and the environment. Control is made possible by empowering the EPA administrator to place restrictions on the production, distribution, use, and disposal of new toxic substances or toxic substances proposed for new applications. Hence, this act provides a mechanism for the creation of specific hazardous waste management regulations for individual substances. Section 6e represents a mandate for promulgation of the first such set of regulations on storage and disposal of a specific hazardous waste, PCB-contaminated materials.

Clean Air Act, Pl 88-206, as Amended

In many respect, this act parallels the federal

Water Pollution Control Act with regard to atmospheric emissions. Regulations are to include the creation of air quality standards and emission control requirements. In this regard, specific rules, guidelines, and regulations will address substances potentially defined as hazardous wastes. Perhaps the greatest area of hazardous waste management impact lies in the control of emission from incinerators and other hazardous waste treatment facilities. As in the case with the water laws, the Clear Air Act creates incentives to reduce residual emission and in so doing creates sludges and other wastes that will be disposed of on land. Many of these wastes are potentially hazardous in nature.

Hazardous Materials Transportation Act, Pl 93-633

This act covers the regulation of labeling and transporting hazardous materials. As such, it address the transportation aspects of hazardous waste management. Potential conflict with RCRA was anticipated by Congress and dealt with through specific instructions in RCRA for the EPA to coordinate all transportation-related regulations with DOT.

Occupational Safety and Health Act, PL 91-596

This act does not address hazardous waste management per se, but all hazardous waste management facilities will have to be operated in compliance with standards focused on worker safety and health.

With the listed pieces of legislation addressing segments of the hazardous waste management problem set, there are many opportunities for overlap and potential inconsistencies. To date, the only safeguards against such problems have been interagency task forces and reviews. Historically, this has been insufficient to provide ample coordination of related regulatory thrusts. As a consequence, the summaries f legislation provided here should not be viewed as illustrative of a comprehensive regulatory net with well-defined interfaces. Rather, the authorities and coverage are confused, and there is great need for a hazardous materials management reform act that would provide a single focal point for cradle-to-grave management of all hazardous substances. This would eliminate replicate definitions (e.g., toxic pollutants, hazardous substances, toxic substances, hazardous wastes, etc), management gaps, conflicting incentives, and multiple regulatory requirements that create unnecessary economic impacts.

Foreign regulatory programs

As one might expect, the extent of hazardous waste management activities outside of the United Stated directly reflects the degree of industrialization and the level of environmental awareness in a given country. Examples range from highly integrated systems well ahead of American practices to minimal programs that do not recognize the existence of special waste categories.

Canadian efforts closely parallel those in many of the individual states in the United

States. The close proximity to the United States and extensive industrial interrelations have made Canadian business a part of the hazardous waste management chain in the United State, both as a source of such wastes and as the operator of treatment and disposal sites. Rising interest in quantifying the management problem and recognition of planning needs have stimulated a flurry of recent activities. There was no comprehensive hazardous waste legislation for all of Canada by 1980. However, through the Environmental contamination ACt, the government does have certain interprovincial authority. Primacy resides with the provinces. The federal government and several provincial governments are conducting studies to inventory wastes and site facilities. Ontario has taken the most extensive action, with a seven-point program that among other things outlaws the disposal of liquid wastes to land. Provincial-owned disposal facilities are being considered. A high degree of interchange between United States and Canadian officials suggests that much of what results from these efforts will closely parallel work in the United States.

Similarly inventory studies have recently been published in Mexico for the area surrounding Mexico City. This work has stirrd public interest, but no specific legislation has been forthcoming. In outlying area, discharge of toxic materials goes on virtually uncontested. Hazardous materials management problems in central America are largely associated with the use and disposal of pesticides. Incidents of acute poisoning in Central America are reported at a rate 2160 times that observed in the United States. No legislation addresses the waste disposal aspects of the problem. Similarly, most South American countries have no specific toxic waste legislation, even though the problems has been clearly identified as a result of incidents such as mercury contamination of the Bay of Castogena and the coastal areas near Moron, Venezuela, Brazil and Argentina have enacted some legislation focusing on discharges to rivers, but effectiveness in hampered by less than vigorous enforcement. For instance, in Brazil, officials of the federal environmental agency have expressed concern that toxic effluents are severely impacting the environment in the northeastern part of the country but that local officials have withheld action for fear of discouraging industrial development. The economic problems of the early 1980s severely hampered efforts to gain tighter control on these problems.

There is still much diversity in the specific legislation and extent of implementation between countries, but a thread of continuity is beginning to develop. Members of the European Community take in to account EC directives when designing new acts. The latter have been instituted to harmonize European legislation and thus stop trade barriers between the states and guarantee acceptable levels of risk within the EC. The council of the EC adapted a directive on toxic and dangerous wastes on March 20, 1978. Members of the Ec has until March 1980 to indicate how they would implement the directive. Heavily concentrated industries and decreasing availability of land for disposal has forced a strong regulatory posture early on. Specific legislation in Britain dates back to 1974 and the Control of Pollution Act. Implementation and enforcement are left to local government, whose charter it is to survey all wastes and arrange for safe disposal. To date, the more relevant aspects of the law have not been implemented. The Poisonous Wastes Act includes the first segments addressing disposal of hazardous wastes on land. consideration of reclamation is mandatory. In addition. The government has established a Waste Management Advisory Council to examine problems associated with recovery of wastes and methods of encouraging reclamation.

Several features of Swedish law closely resemble segments contained in RCRA. Industries are required to report the quantities and content of wastes, and chemical waste transporters and disposers must obtain permits. The federal role is particularly strong, because most wastes are handled by SAKAB, which is 90% state-owned. Although Norwegian industry is responsible for proper management of chemical wastes, environmental authorities assist by collecting wastes and distributing them to commercial treatment plants. Denmark has been a fore-runner in toxic waste management, with pesticide-related regulations dating back to 1953. The major authority for hazardous waste regulations stems from the environmental Protection ACt of 1973. Current laws prohibit direct discharge of rivers or sewers, and above-ground storage is closely controlled. Chemical wastes are collected by municipalities and shipped to a central plant for treatment.

Disposal of waste chemicals and oils in The Netherlands is subject to a series of laws that require generators to deliver wastes only to licensed disposers. The Chemical Wastes Act of 1977 relates to chemical wastes and used oil. The main purpose of this act is to introduce much stricter controls over the transportation, disposal, and treatment of chemical and oily wastes. Nevertheless, the act envisages measures to limit the production of these wastes. These may include regulations requiring a prohibition to manufacture or market certain goods and a prohibition to manufacture or market certain goods if they do not comply with the requirements of a General Administrative Order. Other pertinent acts include the Waste Disposal Act and the Soil Protection Act.

Span has not had active laws in place for hazardous waste management but is in preparation for joining the EC; legislation is being drafted on protection of air, water, and soil quality. This, of necessity, will be designed to meet standards set by the EC. Irish efforts stem from the creation of a task force in April 1971 whose charter would be to investigate problems of waste disposal. A series of reports has resulted from subsequent meetings, along with a recommendation that government become more involved in legislation for disposal and reclamation.

Belgium passed a hazardous waste management act in 1979 and has several active governmental working parties studying specific issues. Further legislation is planned for specific aspects of waste disposal and reclamation. Preliminary indications suggest that, in part, this legislation will establish a joint government-industry company to collect and manage hazardous wastes. Although Luxembourg does not currently have legislation on the books, they historically have followed Belgium's lead.

French efforts began in earnest in 1975 with passage of a law placing management responsibility for dangerous wastes on th generators. Ultimately, a national agency is to be established with a charter for disposal and recycle of wastes. Officials currently have authority to demand waste inventories from generators and require disposal in certified facilities. A national system for toxic waste collection is also under consideration. Although West Germany boasts several very sophisticated waste management facilities, specific regulation is still in the discussion stages. Future activity in Itally is expected to authorize organization of regional toxic waste processing and disposal facilities as a taxed service. In the meantime, Italian industry claims to be increasingly less competitive with other European firms because of stricter constraints on waste management. Swiss law is quite general, prohibiting disposal to stagnant waters or areas of public access.

As in other parts of the world, the recession of the 1980s slowed promulgation of new regulations and decreased enforcement of existing ones. While a number of sites requiring remedial action have been identified, no major program has emerged in any of the European countries to hasten restoration.

Relatively low concentrations of industry in the Middle East and Africa have forestalled public recognition of hazardous waste problems and subsequent legislation. South Africa does boast a fledgling service industry reportedly employing secure landfills, but recent reports question the adequacy of some of the sites being utilized.

Asia offers examples of some of the best and worst of foreign management programs. In India, several major incidents and widespread contamination near metropolitan areas have failed to stimulate definite regulation of dumping or other waste discharge practices. In Bangladesh, programs to provide for secure landfill and resource recovery are under development. The government of Hong Kong has drafted a bill to regulate the disposal of toxic wastes. Chinese efforts to control environmental releases were set back by recent modernization programs. Efforts there, as well as in Japan, Taiwan, and the Philippines, are focused on air and water emissions. Hazardous waste legislation per se has not been developed. Similarly, a recent report by Australian scientists has decried the lack of specific legislation in that country addressing issues of land pollution from waste disposal.

4 Health and Safety Training for Hazardous Waste Activities

A wide array of field activities associated with environmental practice-environmental site assessments, hazardous waste site cleanups, implementing safe storage practices for hazardous materials, conducting emergency response activities in the event of a spill-have a common goal: preventing potentially harmful materials from reaching the general public. However, the most immediately exposed individuals are emergency responders, site investigators, and site cleanup workers. Their protection is critical and begins with health and safety training, i.e., the joining of environmental response with occupational health and safety.

This chapter discusses the various aspects of health and safety training programs for personnel who work with environmental hazards, primarily hazardous waste. The history of hazardous waste training, the training requirements of the Occupational safety and health administration's *Hazardous waste operations and emergency response* standard, and some methods of providing this training are presented. In addition, three types of operations identified by the standard and the different types of training required for each are also addressed. Finally, the establishment of training goals, the development of practical means of delivering the training, and methods of measuring its effectiveness are discussed.

Definitions and explanations

Understanding the training requirements and how they apply to a particular work force requires an understanding of the hazardous waste operations terminology. The terms that follow are used throughout this chapter. Where appropriate, they have been shortened and clarified; complete definitions can be found in the OSHA *Hazardous waste operations and emergency response* standard. For some terms, it is necessary to use the definitions directly from this standard.

- *Buddy system*: A system of organizing personnel into workgroups in such a manner that each employee of the workgroup is designated to be observed by at least one other employee in the workgroup. The purpose of the buddy system is to provide rapid assistance to employees in the event of an emergency.

- *Decontamination*: The removal of hazardous substances from personnel and their equipment to the extent necessary to preclude the occurrence of foreseeable adverse health effects.

- *Emergency response*: A response effort by employees from outside the immediate release area or by other designated responders to an occurrence that results, or is likely to result in, an uncontrolled release of hazardous substances.

- *Hazardous materials response* team: An organized group of employees, designated by the employer, that is expected to control actual or potential leaks or spills of hazardous substances requiring possible close approach to the substance. The team members perform responses to releases or potential releases of hazardous substances for the purpose of control or stabilization of the incident.
- *Hazardous substance:* Any substance designated or listed as noted in the following, exposure to which results or can result in adverse effects on the health or safety of employees:
  - Any substance defined under section 101(14) of the comprehensive environmental response, compensation, and liability act, commonly known as superfund.
  - Any biologic agent and other disease-causing agent that after release into the environment and upon exposure, ingestion, inhalation, or assimilation into any person, either directly from the environment or indirectly by ingestion through food chains, will or can reasonably be anticipated to cause death, disease, behavioral abnormalities, cancer, genetic mutation, physiological

malfunctions, or physical deformations in such persons or their offspring.

— Any substance listed by the U.S. Department of transportation as hazardous material under 49 CFR 172.101.

— Hazardous waste as defined in HAZWOPER.

- Hazardous waste: A waste or combination of wasters as defined in the resource conservation and recovery act, or those substances defined as hazardous wastes in 49 CFR 171.8.
- HAZWOPER: An acronym for Hazardous waste operations and emergency response, *the* OSHA *standard.*
- *Level A protection:* The higher level of protection from chemical hazards,. Known to the media as a "moon suit", it is formally called a "fully encapsulating suit" and includes a supplied-air breathing system. Designed to provide maximum skin and respiratory protection against chemical gases, vapors, and splashes.
- *Level B protection*: The level that uses the supplied-air breathing system for maximum respiratory protection but the protective suit foe splash protection; for example, a cloud of chlorine or other gas could pass through seams or openings in the suit and contact the skin.
- Level C protection: The level C protective suit is similar to that for level B, but the respiratory protection is downgraded to an air-

purifying respirator, which has a number of limitations, particularly in unknown environments.

- *Level D protection:* The level consisting of standard work clothing, e.g., a protective helmet, safety glasses, cotton coveralls, and protective boots, only for use where there are no anticipated chemical hazards to skin or respiratory system.
- *Personal protective equipment*: Specialized clothing, including respirators, that protects the worker from exposure to hazardous chemicals.

History of hazardous waste operations and emergency response training

As it is practiced in the 1990s, most hazardous waste-related health and safety training has its roots in training that was initiated by the environmental protection agency in the late 1970s. A significant portion of this training was aimed at the emergency responder. In the early days of environmental awareness, the emergency responder was frequently involved in operations associated with the investigation of hazardous chemical found at abandoned drum sites, train derailments that included cars of extremely toxic or flammable chemicals, or cleanup of the residue from fires in hazardous waste treatment/storage facilities.

The cornerstone emergency responder course was EPA 165.5, "Hazardous materials incident response organization", which focused on abandoned waste site operations. EPA 165.2, "Personal protection and safety", also provide significant health and safety information to the hazardous waste worker. Each of these courses is still taught in a 40-hour program. Many commercial environmental response and cleanup firms modeled their internal training courses after 165.5 and 165.2.

Unfortunately, since these initial EPA courses were primarily for federal, state, and local personnel and only partially available to workers in the private sector, it was relatively difficult for the latter personnel to obtain the training. A variety of OSHA standards required training for specific activities associated with hazardous waste operations and emergency response. However, the emphasis on training present in today's HAZWOPER standard did not exist then, particularly for personnel involved in site investigation and cleanup activities. Most of the personnel who received EPA training tended to work for the emergency response and site cleanup contractors who worked closely with or were under contract to EPA and state environmental agencies. Therefore, less training was available for other personnel working at hazardous waste sites.

The training issue was brought to the attention of congress, and a response was provided in section 126 of the superfund amendments and reauthorization act of 1986, which was signed into law on October 17, 1986. OSHA was directed to:

issue an interim final rule within 60 days after the date of enactment, which specified providing no less protection for workers engaged in covered operations than the protections contained in the environmental protection agency's "Health and safety requirements for employees engaged in field activities" manual dated 1981 and the existing OSHA standards under subpart C to 29 CFR 1926.

In response, OSHA *issued* Hazardous waste operations and emergency response; interim final rule on December 19, 1986.

OSHA borrowed heavily from existing documents, particularly the previously mentioned EPA 1440.2, as well as the joint NIOSH/OSHA/U.S. Coast guard/EPA document entitled Occupational safety and health guidance manual for hazardous waste site activities, *a 1985* manual that continues to be used extensively today. While the final standard was not to be promulgated until March 6, 1989, SARA required the interim final rule to take effect upon issuance; therefore, initial training requirements, as well as several other requirements, were to be fully implemented by March 16, 1987.

When SARA was amended in 1987, congress directed OSHA to develop specific procedures for the accreditation of hazardous waste operation training programs that are no less comprehensive than those adopted by EPA under the Asbestos Hazard Emergency Response Act. Under the proposed rules, which will become 29 CFR 1910.121 when finalized, OSHA would set up a program to review training materials and trainer qualifications, and confer accreditation on those firms that met certain criteria. In addition, the proposed rules specify minimum subject requirements for various types of training courses. As of january 1994, the fate of this standard is in doubt; however, the minimum subject criteria have come into wide usage.

Establishing the training program

Personnel cannot take part in any type of hazardous waste-related activity unity they have successfully completed the required training. The initial step in establishing a program that will provide the required training is to perform a needs assessment. The employer should first confirm that the personnel will be participating in operations that are covered by the HAZWOPER standard. However, one should resist the temptation to assume that if the particular operation is in a "gray area" not directly covered by the standard, no training is required.

Employers will frequently use HAZWOPER training as a "catch all" to try to cover all applicable OSHA requirements. Actually, the minimum training under HAZWOPER must often be tailored to include requirements of the other applicable standards, or the initial training must be augmented with additional sessions that include employer-specific information. This is an important concept that must be understood and incorporated into all training, as will be demonstrated in the subsequent sections of this chapter.

Once it has been established that the employer's personnel will be required to participate in activities that are impacted by HAZWOPER, the proper type of training then be selected. The goals of training for employees involved in any type of hazardous waste activity are;

- to make workers aware of the potential hazards they may encounter
- to provide the knowledge and skill necessary to perform the work with minimal risk to worker health and safety
- to make workers aware of the purpose and limitations of safety equipment
- to ensure that workers can safely avoid or escape emergencies.

Such goals must be closely aligned with the training course selected for an employer's hazardous waste personnel.

Initial training

There are three distinct types of activities under HAZWOPER that require initial training.

- cleanup operations at hazardous waste sites, including initial investigations
- hazardous waste operations at permitted and interim status RCRA treatment, storage, and disposal facilities
- emergency response operations.

Cleanup operations

If the needs assessment indicates that affected personnel will participate in site investigation or cleanup operations, the employer has to consider two more issues: (1) will the employee's job function present potential exposure to health and safety hazards associated with hazardous waste activities? If so, (2) which type of investigation/ cleanup activities will each employee be involved in?

A representative interpretive response from OSHA indicated that workers are not covered by HAZWOPER, and, therefore, not subject to the training requirements, if they;

- work exclusively within uncontaminated areas of the hazardous waste site
- do not enter areas where hazardous waste may exist, is stored, or is processed
- are not exposed to health or safety hazards related to hazardous waste operations.

Examples of this situation include clerical staff who work in the site office trailer located outside of the contaminated area, personnel engaged in construction activities in uncontaminated areas of the site, or a truck driver who delivers a load of fill material to a location outside of the contaminated are. Note that OSHA may require the employer to establish that such work areas are in fact of contamination. Such personnel should be trained in site emergency response procedures in the event that there is a release of hazardous substances requiring an evacuation.

Once it is established that personnel do have to be trained, the employer must decide what type of initial training is required, i.e., 40-hour or 24-hour. In general, 40-hour training is for workers who will be or can exposed to uncontrolled or uncharacterized hazardous substances and their associated health hazards; 24-hour training is for personnel who work in areas that have been fully characterized as to the type of hazards present, and for which air monitoring has established that it is unlikely that such personnel will be exposed to airborne substances over the occupational exposure limits.

For all practical purposes, the difference between 40-hour and 24-hour training is that the latter does not provide training in respiratory protection or high-hazard operations. By definition, personnel in areas of high hazard or chemical exposure potential. If such personnel are later required to work in uncharacterized or high-hazard areas, they must first complete the additional 16 hours of training to bring them up to "40-hour status." Many environmental consulting firms do not use the 24-hour option foe their field personnel because it limits flexibility in task assignment. However, 24-hour training may be useful and cost-effective for personnel with task-specific, long-term assignments.

The HAZWOPER standard provides broad, general requirements for both 40- and 24-hour training course contents. HAZWOPER is designed to be a "performance standard," that is, the employer designs the various aspects of the program within the context of the specific requirements of the standard to address the health and safety hazards particular to the employer's operation. OSHA is emphatic that the level of training provided be consistent with the worker's job function and responsibilities. This is evident when viewing the training elements of HAZWOPER.

- names of personnel and alternates responsible for site safety and health
- safety, health, and other hazards present on the site
- use of personnel protective equipment
- work practices by which we employee can minimize risks from hazards
- safe use of engineering controls and equipment on the site
- medical surveillance requirements, including recognition of symptoms and signs that might indicate overexposure to the hazards
- information from the site health and safety plan, including;
  - — decontamination procedures
  - — emergency response plan
  - — confined space entry procedures
  - — spill containment program

Note that there is an assumption that the training will be designed to be site specific. Such 40- or 24-hour training is the exception rather than the rule, because rarely can an employer anticipate which employees will be assigned to a specific site or in fact anticipate what the employee's first assignment will be. Therefore, moist initial training programs are not site specific; rather, most issues are covered in a generic sense, addressing, for example a model emergency response plan or a typical confined space entry procedure. Under these circumstances, it is the employer's responsibility under this performance standard to see that the workers receive additional site-and task-specific training as part of the three days of on-the-job training prior to commencing site work.

The proposed training accreditation standard, which was previously discussed, describes minimum criteria and content for training programs that OSHA will require in order to consider them as acceptable for accreditation. These criteria are much more detailed than those provided in HAZWOPER. Various training and hazardous materials consulting firms have adopted these criteria as the working outlines foe their training course.

Treatment, storage, and disposal facilities

Treatment, storage, and disposal facility personnel are already subject to training requirements prescribed by the EPA in 40 CFR 264 and 265; such requirements can be readily woven into the HAZWOPER requirements. As with cleanup operations. the employer must determine whether the particular TSDF is exempted from these requirements; such exemptions are usually associated with "conditionally exempt small quantity generators." Employers should review the "Notes and exceptions" portion of 29 CFR 1910.120 (a) (2) to see whether this exemption applies. New TSDF employees must complete 24 hours of initial training in order to "perform their assigned duties and functions in a safe and healthful manner so as not endanger themselves or other employees."

Current employers of a TSDF for whom the employer can establish previous training and experience equivalent to the 24-hour initial training do not have to take the training. However, "current employee" may be interpreted as being in the position prior to the March 9, 1990, effective date of the HAZWOPER final standard, so one may not wish to read too much into this equivalency provision.

HAZWOPER is vague regarding the specific elements that the 24-hour TSDF course should cover.

It is implied that it will cover the elements of the required health and safety program. identification evaluation, and control of safety and health hazards; emergency response criteria; waste-handling procedures; maximum exposures limits; and engineering controls. Also included is hazard communication training, medical surveillance, decontamination, and materials handling. Fortunately, the proposed 1910.121 cuts through all the vagueness and describes what

OSHA would really like to see in a TSDF curriculum.

- Overview of the applicable paragraphs of 29 CFR 1910.120 and the elements of an employer's effective occupational safety and heal;the program and those responsible for the program.
- Overview of relevant hazards such as, but not limited to, chemical exposures, biological exposures, fire and explosion exposures, radiological exposures, and heat and cold exposures.
- General safety hazards including those associated with electrical hazards, powered equipment, and walking-working surfaces.
- Confined space hazards and procedures (now addressed by 29 CFR 1910.146).
- Work practice that will minimize employee risk from workplace hazards.
- A review of the employer's hazardous waste-handling procedures, including the materials handling program and spill containment program.
- An overview and explanation of the employer's Hazard communication program meeting the requirements of 29 CFR 1910.1200 for those chemicals other than hazardous waste in the workplace.
- A review of the employer's medical surveillance programs meeting the

requirements of 29 CFR, including the recognition of signs and symptoms of overexposures to relevant hazardous substances.

- A review of the employer's training program and the personnel responsible for that program.
- A review of the employer's personal protective equipment program, including the proper selection and use of PPE based upon specific site hazards.
- Safe use of engineering controls and equipment.
- A review of the applicable appendixes to 29 CFR 1910.120.
- Principles of toxicology and biological monitoring.
- Rights and responsibilities of employees and employers under OSHA and RCRA.
- Sources of reference and efficient use of relevant manuals and knowledge of hazard coding systems.
- Hands-on exercises and demonstrations with equipment excepted to be used during the performance of work duties.
- Final examination.

Throughout this curriculum descriptions, OSHA refers to the employer's programs or procedures.

More than for the other two types of training,

initial training for TSDF personnel can and should be facility-specific. This is because at the completion of the training, employees will be working in one particular facility.

TSDF employees who are to participate in facility emergency response activities are to receive additional training in the elements of the employer's emergency response plan and other issues.

Emergency response operations

In both hazardous waste cleanup operations and TSDF training, personnel must be oriented to emergency response procedures in the event that an emergency does occur at their site; however, the emphasis is on health and safety associated with normal site operations. Traditional emergency responses, on the other hand, can face a different situation every time they respond. To address this, OSHA has developed five ER training categories, each accompanied by a different set of training requirements. The employer should consider the following OSHA training categories when developing the emergency response team and assigning personnel to emergency responder tasks.

First responder awareness level. First responders at the awareness level are individuals who are likely to witness or discover a hazardous substance release and who have ben trained to initiate an emergency response sequence by notifying the authorities of the release.

First responder operations level. First responders at the operations level are individuals who respond to releases or potential releases of hazardous substances as part of the initial response to the site for the purpose of protecting nearby persons, property, or the environment from the effects of the release. They are trained to respond in a defensive fashion without actually trying to stop the release. Their function is to contain the release from a safe distance, keep it from spreading, and prevent exposures.

Hazardous materials technician. Hazardous materials technicians are individuals who respond to releases or potential release situations for the purpose of preventing or stopping the release. They assume a more aggressive role than a first responder at the operations level in that they will approach the point of release in order to plug, patch, or otherwise stop the release of a hazardous substance.

Hazardous materials specialist. Hazardous materials specialists are individuals who respond with and provide support to hazardous materials technicians. Their duties parallel those of the hazardous materials technician; however, those duties require a more specific knowledge of the various substances they may be called upon to contain. The hazardous materials specialist would also act as the site liaison with federal, state, local, and other government authorities regarding site activities.

On-scene incident commander. Incident commanders assume control of the incident scene beyond the first responder awareness level. OSHA defines the "on-scene incident commander" as the "most senior official on site who has the responsibility for controlling the operation at the site." Such senior officials may be a battalion chief, fire chief, state law enforcement official, or site coordinator. All emergency responders and their communications are to be coordinated and controlled through the on-scene incident commander assisted by the senior official present for each employer.

In contrast to hazardous waste cleanup and TSDF operations, in which the HAZWOPER standard and the proposed training certification standard essentially state what topics must be included in a training program, emergency responders have topic areas in which they must "demonstrate competency." OSHA does not address the training of emergency responders in the proposed 29 CFR 1910.121, stating that it would not be effective to try to certify all the fire agencies throught the country who provide emergency response services. Clearly, OSHA expects the training curriculum to be tailored to anticipated response activities, and notes that training is required for those who participate or *who are expected to participate* in emergency response.

OSHA's performance goals for the five ER training categories are discussed next. Representative training topics as found in some commercial training programs are included where appropriate.

Performance goals: emergency responders

First responders at the awareness level shall have sufficient training or have had sufficient experience to objectively demonstrate competency in the following areas:

- understanding hazardous substances and the risks associated with them in a incident
- understanding the potential outcomes associated with an emergency created when hazardous substances are present
- recognizing the presence of hazardous substances in an emergency
- identifying the hazardous substances, if possible
- understanding the role of the first responder awareness individual in the employer's emergency response plan, site security and control, and the U.S. department of transportation's *emergency response guidebook*
- realizing the need for additional resources and making appropriate notifications to the communication center.

The employer shall certify that first responders at the operational level have received at least eight hours of training or have sufficient experience to objectively demonstrate competency and receive employer certification in the following areas in addition to those listed for the awareness level;

- basic hazard and risk assessment techniques
- selecting and using proper personal protective

equipment provided to the first responder operational level

- basic hazardous materials terms
- performing basic control, containment, and/or confinement operations within the capabilities of the resources and personal protective equipment available with their unit
- implementing basic decontamination procedures
- relevant standard operating procedures and termination procedures.

Representative training topics include:

- Regulatory requirements
- Toxicology
- Industrial Hygiene
- Decontamination
- Spill Control Practicum
- Chemistry of Hazardous Substances
- Hazardous Chemical Workshop
- Personal Protective Equipment
- Spill Control Techniques.

The employer shall certify that hazardous materials technicians have received at least 24 hours of training equal to the first responder operations level and in addition demonstrate competency and receive employer certification in the following areas:

- implementing the employer's emergency response plan
- classification, identification, and verification of known and unknown materials by using field survey instruments and equipment
- function within an assigned role in the incident command system
- selecting and using proper specialized chemical personal protective equipment provided to the hazardous materials technician
- hazard and risk assessment techniques
- performing advance control, containment, and/or confinement operations within the capabilities of the resources and personal protective equipment available with the unit
- understanding and implementing decontamination procedures
- understanding termination procedures
- understanding basic chemical and toxicological terminology and behavior.

Representative training topics include:

- Regulatory requirements
- Toxicology
- Protective clothing
- Medical surveillance
- Physical hazards
- Site control methods

- Contingency planning
- Incident command systems
- Chemical hazards
- Air monitoring instruments
- Respiratory protection
- Decontamination procedures
- Safe work practices
- Site safety plans
- Materials handling techniques
- Field practicum.

The employer shall certify that hazardous materials specialists have competency in the following areas:

- implementing the local emergency response plan
- classification, identification, and verification of known and unknown materials by using advanced survey instrument and equipment
- state emergency response plan
- selecting and using proper specialized chemical personal protective equipment provided to the hazardous materials specialist
- in-depth hazards and risk assessment techniques
- performing specialized control, containment, and/or confinement operations within the capabilities of the resources and personal protective equipment available

- determining and implementing decontamination procedures
- developing a site safety and control plan
- chemical, radiological, and toxicological terminology and behavior.
- training topics for hazardous materials specialists would be similar to those for hazardous materials technicians.

The employer shall certify that incident commanders have received at least 24 hours of training equal to the first responder operations level and, in addition, have competency in the following areas:

- implementing the employer's incident command system
- implementing the employer's emergency response plan
- hazards and risks associated with employees working in chemical protective clothing
- implementing the local emergency response plan
- knowledge of state emergency response plan and of the Federal Regional Response Team
- importance of decontamination procedures

Representative training topics include:

- Regulatory requirements
- State ER plans
- Decontamination

- ICS Operating requirements
- Organization and Operations
- Personal protective equipment
- Emergency response planning
- Contingency planning
- Hazardous material recognition
- Factors affecting emergency management
- Media management
- ICS Workshop.

OSHA provides an interesting training exemption for what it calls "skilled support personnel." These are personnel, such as equipment operators, who have skills that are needed immediately and who will be exposed to sit hazards, but who have not had emergency response training. Skilled support personnel do not need to complete the training, but they must have an initial briefing prior to commencing work. It is clear that as soon as properly trained personnel are available to take the place of the skilled support personnel, the latter are to be removed from the hazard area.

Refersher training

Once initial training is completed, additional training requirements must be considered. all three training categories require personnel to complete an annual "refresher" training course. Refresher training provides an opportunity to reemphasize important points and review actual incidents to evaluate lessons learned. Both

Hazards Waste Operations and TSDF personnel must complete an eight-hour refresher course annually. Refresher course requirements and accreditation are specifically excluded from the proposed 29 CFR 1910.121. The HAZWOPER standard specifies that the Hazardous waste Operations refresher course shall review the topics presented in the initial training course and critique incidents that provide training example of related work. The standard does not specify curriculum for the TSDF personnel.

Emergency response personnel are to "receive annual refresher training of sufficient content to maintain their competencies, or shall demonstrate competency in those areas at least yearly." the number of hours and type of topics for his refresher course are not specified.

Refresher courses can be accomplished in several ways. Typically, the employer provides an eight-hour classroom session once a year. However, many employers with employees assigned to only one location for the year may schedule periodic "brown bag" training sessions to cover refresher topics. One alternate method is to hold a one-hour session every month, documenting that each employee attends at least eight sessions per year.

The employer must consider what is meant by "annual," for it may very among federal OSHA and the various state program OSHA agencies. A federal OSHA interpretation of the standard states that "OSHA's intent is that employees should complete their refresher training within twelve months of their initial training," and if a course is missed, the employee should take the next available course. the interpretation notes that some states require the refresher to be completed by the exact anniversary date of the initial training. At least one state requires initial training to be retaken if the employee does not take a refresher within two years of the anniversary date of the initial training or previous refresher. Note that under similar circumstances federal OSHA requires only that the employee "demonstrate competency" but does recommend retraining if the employee has been away from the field for a significant amount of time.

Supervisor training

Supervisor training is required of hazardous waste operations on-site managers and supervisors who are directly responsible for, or who supervise employees engaged in, hazardous waste operations. This is generally intepreted to include at least the site manager and the site safety officer; more people may be included for larger, more people may be included for larger, more complex sites. HAZWOPER requires that supervisors receive the initial training described earlier, as well as eight hours of specialized training on the following topics.

- the employer's safety and health program, and the associated employee training program
- personnel protective equipment

- spill containment program
- health hazard monitoring procedures and techniques.

The proposed 29 CFR 1910.121 added;

- management of hazardous wastes and their disposal
- federal, state, and local agencies to be contacted in the event of a release of hazardous substances
- management of emergency procedures in the event of a release of hazardous substances.

Although this is a good beginning for an SSO, it is insufficient for someone who is responsible foe health and safety activities at a complex site. Tables 9-g and 9-h describe two approaches to certifying an SSO for various types of hazardous waste site operations.

Supervisor training must also be refreshed annually, which could lead an employer to assume that two separate refresher courses must be conducted each year. A careful evaluation of 29 CFR 1910.120(e)(8), which describes supervisor training requirements, states that employees who have received initial training and supervisors who have received supervisor training have to be refreshed annually on the topics of initial training "and/or" the topics of supervisor training. Therefore, only one annual refresher course need be held, but it must contain components of both initial and supervisor training if supervisory personnel are in attendance.

Supervised field experience

For employees engaged in hazardous waste operation, the initial 24 or 40 hours of off-site training must be followed up by supervised field experience. Such field experience must be completed prior to the employee independently engaging in field operations. For personnel with 24 hours of initial training a minimum of one day pf actual field experience is required; for employees with 40 hours of initial training, minimum of three days of actual field experience must be completed. Such field experience must be conducted under the supervision of a trained, experienced supervisor.

The purpose of supervised field experience is clear. Classroom training, even with a comprehensive field practicum, does not, by itself, adequately prepare personnel foe hazardous waste field activities. One must learn to use protective equipment and monitoring equipment under actual field conditions in order to function as an effective team member.

The employee's field experience should use the level of protection that the employee will be expected to use during independent project operations. It does no good to complete the supervised field experience in level D protection, then expect the employee to be able to function effectively in level B the following week. It is therefore recommended that employees receive three days of supervised field experience in each of the levels of protection in which they will be expected to work.

If an employee with experience in levels D and C is assigned to a level B project, then the first three days of work should be supervised field experience. Note that this may not be required if an employees is downgrading the level of protection, such as receiving field experience in level B, then being assigned to level D. All supervised field training should be documented in writing and a copy placed in the employee's personnel file.

Equivalent training

The initial and/or supervisor training requirements is waived if employers if hazardous waste operations personnel establish that an employee's work experience and/or training is equivalent to the initial training and/or supervisor training required by the standard. The standard states "Equivalent training includes any academic training or the training that existing employees might already have received from actual hazardous waste work experience."

Unfortunately, this paragraph is easily misunderstood and readily misused. Some trainers have given 24 hours of classroom training, then accounted for 16 more hours by certifying various types of field experience as "equivalent" in an attempt to side-step the required additional classroom training. Other similar abuses have occurred. However, in a correction to the HAZWOPER final rule that was published in the Federal register on April 18, 1991, OSHA stated "SARA provides that the required training can result from a course and on the job training or from training and experience prior to the effective date of the interim standard". Because the effective date of the interim standard was April 1987, it would appear that any training or experience obtained after that date may be unacceptable for equivalency.

Conducting the training

For most employers, determining whether HAZWOPER training is required for employees is the easy part; developing and implementing the training program is the real work.

The first order of business is to decide whether to do the training "in-house" or to retain an outside consultant to conduct the training. The development of training curriculum, particularly for the longer, more involved 24- or 40-hour course is time-consuming when it is done correctly. For employers with a large number of personnel involved in hazardous waste operations and emergency response, and who have a health and safety professional on staff, it might be reasonable to do some or most of the training in-house. Some firms will use outside consultants for the 24-or 40-hour courses, and do the eight-hour courses, such as the refresher and supervisor courses, in-house. Most small employers, or those with few employees under HAZWOPER, tend to use outside provides exclusively.

In-house training considerations

If the decision is to do some or all of the applicable training courses in-house, the employer next has to appoint someone to be responsible for developing and conducting the courses. For hazardous waste and TSDF operations, the appropriates choice is an experienced health and safety professional who is familiar with the operations of concern. For example, although fire fighters who are experienced in emergency response can be used for emergency response training, they should be assisted by broadly experienced health and safety professionals. The worst possible approach is to send someone to take the needed course, and after their return have them photocopy the course materials and become the duly appointed trainer.

Logistics is an important issues. If an employer has multiple locations, is it feasible to transport the trainers and/or the trainees to the training site? A significant amount of equipment is used in teaching a 40-hour operations or 24-hour emergency response course. If the employer has a single facility, logistics may not be a deciding factor.

If conducting internal training seems like a good idea, the employer should use the criteria in the following section to fully evaluate the feasibility of this potentially complex undertaking.

Components of a good training course

There are several issues to consider in the selection of a training course provider. Unfortunately, the criteria that are most readily discernable and that may be of primary interest to the unsophisticated employer may be the least reliable indicators of course quality and applicability. One such criterion is price per student. Although price is an important consideration, it is more important to get a quality training program that fulfills OSHA requirements. Experience has indicated that high prices don't necessarily make a good course, and the low bidder may actually conduct a good course. The higher-priced firm with the glossy brochure may have mediocre training personnel, whereas the low-priced university may be subsidized by a grant. However, to compare several provides, the highest priced and the lowest priced should probably be closely evaluated. Managers should compare the offerings with the criteria listed in this section and, before deciding, ask for and check references regarding course value and quality.

Instructors

The quality of instruction is obviously closely tied to the quality of the course instructors. An employer is well-advised to carefully examine the credentials of the instructors. Not all teachers of HAZWOPER courses are equal in skill level or instructional experience. OSHA requires that, for hazardous waste operations courses,

> Trainers shall be qualified to instruct employees about the subject matter that is being presented in training. Such trainers shall have satisfactorily completed a training program for teaching the subjects they are expected to teach, or they shall have the academic credentials and

instructional experience necessary for teaching the subjects. Instructors shall demonstrate competent instructional skills and knowledge of the applicable subject matter.

It may not be easy for the employer to determine whether the instructors meet OSHA's criteria.

For hazardous waste operations and TSDF courses, the course director and/or lead instructor should be a health and safety professional. In the compliance guidelines for HAZWOPER, OSHA recommends that the development and implementation of the site safety and health program be conducted by professional safety and health personnel, such as certified safety professionals, certified industrial hygienists, and registered professional safety engineers. This recommendation should be extended to the development and implementation of training courses. Until 29 CFR 1910.121, which certifies training programs, is promulgated, the use of professional safety and health personnel in training is one of the most readily identifiable assurance of trainer competence.

For emergency response trainers, HAZWOPER makes a very specific requirement for trainer qualification;

Trainers who teach any of the emergency response subjects shall have satisfactorily completed a training course for teaching the subjects they are expected to teach, such as the courses offered by the U.S. National fire academy, or they shall have the training and/or academic credentials and instructional experience necessary to demonstrate competent instructional skills and a good command of the subject matter of the courses they are teach.

Therefore, fire academy credentials would be a good start toward identifying a competent emergency response trainer; beyond that, it become a matter of evaluating field and instructional experience in combination with academic credentials in determining trainer competence.

Training experience is not necessarily interchangeable among the three categories of courses. Fire fighters with emergency response experience probably have little experience relative to hazardous waste operations; conversely, the CIH skilled in hazardous waste operations may not have appropriate material for incident command systems or "plug and patch" activities. Unfortunately, some training provides use the same trainers regardless of the course; if the trainers are not thoroughly experienced in all the areas in which they instruct, the credibility and effectiveness of the course suffers greatly.

Although it is not unreasonable to have one instructor teach an 8-hour session, such as supervisor or refresher, it is an unusual individual who can do an adequate job "going solo" for an entire 24-or 40-hour course, It is unrealistic to ask an instructor to teach the entire session. Instructors will fatigue, students will get bored listening to the same person for a week, and the quality of the course inevitably suffers. A good 40-hour course needs at least two, and preferably three, instructors, whereas a 24-hour offering should have two trainers.

Supporting materials and media

Proper use of supproting materials can have a significant impact on the effectiveness of a presentation. Straight lecture for even eight hours will usually result in boredom and poor retention. Eight hours of videos typically creates the same result. Effective instructors will efficiently blend supporting materials into the lecture to deliver a well-balanced course that fosters a high level of retention by the trainees.

Several firms provide high-quality health and safety videos, many of which are specifically designed to address HAZWOPER issues. The typical video runs from 15 to 25 minutes, so it is not unreasonable to show three or four relevant videos during an eight-hour session. For example, in refresher training, a pretest on a subject can be given prior to showing the video, with answers and discussion to follow. The test questions should be geared to the video so the trainees will be "watching" for the correct solutions.

Trainees also respond to well-designed transparencies, such as those that provide topical outlines of the subject under discussion. These can help keep the discussion focused and lead it toward the desired conclusion. Some trainers will include copies of the transparencies in the course manual, with sufficient blank space to permit the trainees to take notes under the topical headings.

Whenever possible, the instructor should have examples of equipment and protective clothing available during the lecture. Few things better help a trainee retain information than being able to visualize the item under discussion. The various types of classes require different types of "show-and-tell" items, such as respirators and cartridges, gloves, chemical-restraint suits, air-monitoring instruments, plug and patch kits, samples containers, labels, and the like. If the items are small and lightweight, they can be passed around the room. Larger items should be placed where trainees can examine them during a break.

Also effective is the "magic show," in which the instructor demonstrates the reactions that can occur when small quantities of incompatible chemicals are mixed. Popular combinations are combustible liquids with oxidizers and acids with bases. Such exercises must be conducted in a well-ventilated space using the smallest quantities of chemicals that will create a visible reaction. Instructors and participants must take care to avoid mixtures that will create a toxic reaction by-product and potentially generate a hazardous waste.

The course manual is arguably the most important supporting item, because it will be retained by the trainees for future reference. It is time-consuming to develop a high-quality course manual, and unfortunately, some commercial courses show their lack of commitment by simply photocopying and binding together various government documents. Although some of these documents are excellent "stand-alone" resources, they tend not to flow well when scrambled together. A good manual augments original narrative text with charts, graphs, and excerpts from the better government documents.

Employers who are designing their own training program should take advantage of the wealth of information available on hazardous waste operations and emergency response. Many of the resources listed in the references section at the end of this chapter are from appendix D of HAZWOPER.

Exercises

There are three basic types of training exercises that trainers should consider using when developing or evaluating a training course; (1) written classroom exercises, such as the development of a simple contingency or health and safety plan; (2) hands-on classroom exercises, such as monitoring instrument calibration or respirator fit-testing; and (3) field practicums, such as setting up work zones and a decontamination line or suiting up for simulated drum sampling or tank-patching exercises.

A 24-hour course should have each of these types of exercises included in the curriculum. Field practicums are labor-intensive; one instructor can't do it alone. Thus, practicums require a lot of equipment, but there is no better way to equate the classroom lessons with field operations. Some 40-hour courses have one full day dedicated to exercises, starting with the development of a health and safety plan in the classroom. then implementing the plan in field exercises; other courses build through the week to the field practicums as the culminating experience.

Another type of exercise that is effective in shorter courses, particularly in refresher courses in which trainees should already be familiar with the material, is opening each topic with a short quiz, then holding open discussion to answer the questions. Such discussion encourages participation, and lets trainees bring out their personal experiences for others to learn from.

Measuring understanding: exams and field practicums

It is essential for employers and trainers to measure the trainees' understanding of the course material. This will help the trainer evaluate the effectiveness of the course, because if q large percentage of the trainees miss a particular test question, there could have been a problem in delivering the material. For the employer, establishing a means of measuring understanding can limit liability exposures in the event of an injury or illness on the job.

All courses should culminate in an examination that reflects the materials presented. Forty-hour courses may have exams of 100 or more questions, whereas the 8-hour courses may features exams of 40 or 50 questions. Although there is a statistical method for establishing a passing rate for a particular examination, most trainers establish a cutoff at 70% correct answers; a trainee with a score below 70 must either retake the course or undertake remedial studies prior to being certified. Examination cover sheets should have the trainee's name, date, social security number, and signature.

Some of the more sophisticated training providers also score the field practicums. Of course, this adds to an already labor-intensive exercise, but objective scoring can be a valuable tool.

Effective training records can be of great assistance in defending against injury and illness claims. For that reason, many employers are creating employee records of training, in which the employee certifies that certain training was received an understood. When used in conjunction with examination results, such records can assist an employer in establishing that an employee received an understood training that was designed to prevent occupational injuries and illnesses.

Once the classroom sessions, field practicums, and examinations are finished, HAZWOPER requires that successful participants be issued certificates of completion. The certificate must describe the specific type of training provided and state the name of the trainee and course instructor of head instructor. Although not specifically required by the standard, it makes sense to include the date of the training, the name of the firm providing the training, and the location of the course. Many trainers include the trainee's social security number on the certificate as a unique identifier for tracking purposes.

International perspective

Hazardous waste activities are not unique to the United States. European nations, for example, are actively identifying and investigating hazardous waste sites; it appears that sites recently revealed in Eastern Europe will be particularly hazardous. Few countries have health and safety regulations similar in scope to HAZWOPER. However, m,any countries do have standards that reflect those seen in table 9-a, which provide some impetus to conduct HAZWOPER-type training. Some American-based firms have undertaken training programs foe their foreign-based personnel. Although it is possible, and indeed appropriates, for such programs to be conducted, the logistics associated with these activities can be daunting, particularly moving training equipment through customs in a timely fashion. Nevertheless, responsible employers will continue to provide employee engaged in international hazardous waste operations.

Once sites were identified, the program was further charged with these additional tasks:

- provide a mechanism to clean the released substances where there is a risk to public health or the environment

- ensure a site is either cleaned up by responsible parties or the government, where appropriate
- evaluate damages to natural resources from identified releases
- establish a claims procedure for parties that have either spent money to restore natural resources or have cleaned up sites.

Clearly, a strong emphasis was place on the identification of potentially responsible parties for cost recovery. Not surprisingly, the first five years of Superfund were hallmarked by substantial litigation about th implementation and constitutionality of the statute.

In 1986, Superfund was reauthorized by Congress, under a five-year extension known as the Superfund Amendments and Reauthroization Act. The 1993/94 Congress is again faced with reauthorization of Superfund and significant changes have been proposed. Three trends toward streamlining the Superfund process are evident:

- changing the joint and several liability provisions of the law, i.e., everyone is not equally liable financially regardless of the quantity of waste contributed to a site
- modifying the risk assessment process so it is less conservative and produces more technically achievable cleanup levels
- decreasing the amount of time and money directed toward litigation among PRPs and the various federal and state agencies.

Public disenchantment with Superfund is significant, because the perception is that more money has been spent on litigation and study than actual cleanup. In addition, the EPA has become sensitized to th issues of environmental equity and racism. The number of Superfund sites appear to be disproportionately located near or potentially impact poor and/or minority communities. In February 1994, President Clinton signed an executive order mandating greater emphasis on issues of environmental equity.

Spill assessment: General considerations

Spill assessment refers to the steps taken to identify and plan an appropriate response to a spill, and report spills to the regulatory authority. Assessment of spills and releases is initiated as soon as discovery. The scope of an assessment varies with the situation, but the components of the assessment never change. The three steps of a spill assessment are as follows:

1. defining the problem
2. planning appropriate action
3. implementing agency notification and reporting requirements as necessary.

The first tow components must be considered prior to controlling the spill to ensure that control activities are conducted safety, quickly, and effectively. The third component is necessary to meet government requirements and must be performed either during spill control for dangerous spills or before spill control for small nonhazardous spills.

Defining the problem or potential problems: Problem definition is completed by identifying the source and size of the spill or threat of a spill and identifying the materials or waste used at the facility and/or spill. An inventory of raw materials, products used, and generated wastes at the facility should be complied; information, material safety data sheets and information from sampling can be helpful. The toxic, reactive, corrosive, ignitable substances should be identified.

In general, two categories of spills occur at most facilities;

- small nonhazardous or otherwise nonreportable spills that can be cleaned up immediately with no harm to human health or the environment
- spills of hazardous materials that have the potential to harm human health and/ or the environment.

Typically, most large facilities have emergency preparedness teams and environmental coordinators who assess types of spills and determine appropriate response and notification requirements.

The first category of spills or leaks would best fit under good housekeeping procedures. However, it is mentioned here to stress that small leaks and spills can and do result in major environmental problems. Recurring spills or leaks must be reported to the EC so appropriate changes or follow-up action can take place. Examples of this type of spill care:

- fuel spilled at fuel island
- small spills of dry chemical, cement, and sand that accumulate on the yard.
- spills from vendor tankers, fill lines, or discharge hoses
- oil-stained solid around maintenance shop oil tanks.

The second category of spills must be immediately reported to the dispatcher by the person who discovers or causes the spill. Examples of this type of spill include:

- significant leaks of acid due to storage tank valve failure
- field waste drain plugs that cause field wastes to overflow to soil
- acid wastewater or field wastes to overflow because of rain.

To help an owner/operator define and evaluate the problem, the following list of questions has been developed;

- Is the materials spilled hazardous?
- What was spilled?
- Was anyone hurt?
- Is medical assistance needed?
- Is any person, group, or community in danger?
- Is there any danger of fire, explosion, or air quality problems?

- What was the source of the spill?
- Has the source of the spilled material been stopped?
- Is the spilled material flowing off the site?
- Has the spilled material been contained?
- How much material was spilled?

The answer to these questions will be the basis for initial response action. Planning appropriate action. The second part of spill assessment involves decisions about how to handle the different types of spills that could occur at the facility. The procedures for internal notification are as important as external notification. Typically, a dispatcher has the first role in this decision-making process. Based on the information provided during the initial spill notification, the dispatcher determines the "first" level of response necessary for each type of the incident and immediately contracts the responsible party. The "first" level refers to the "first" call the dispatcher makes after receiving the spill notification. If there is a fire, explosion, injured individuals, or other life-threatening situations, then the "first" call is directed to fire of ambulance services.

In all other cases, the dispatcher initially contacts the EC or the EPT to assist in the spill assessment. Usually, senior supervisory personnel are in the responsible positions. These people are available for guidance in nonemergency situations and are often the most knowledgeable of facility processes, potential problem areas, and substances used at the facility.

For all chemical, fuel, or waste spills except for small nonhazardous spills, the dispatcher should contact appropriate management immediately after the EC or EPT has been contracted.

Assigned personnel are responsible for planning small nonhazardous spills, the dispatcher should contact appropriate management immediately after the EC to EPT has been contracted.

Assigned personnel are responsible for planning and implementing the appropriate response actions for each reported spill. These actions vary widely based on the size, nature, and complexity of the spill.

The response actions may include:

- minor cleanups from small spills with no notification
- calling for additional outside assistance
- notifying federal, state, and local agencies
- isolating the area and setting up work zones
- controlling and cleaning up the spill
- protecting personnel during cleanup
- disposing of waste materials properly
- restoring the spill area and spill equipment.

Notification and reporting requirements. When a spill occurs, the EC to EPT must decide whether agencies are to be notified regarding the type of spill. Reporting requirements are triggered by releasing into the environment, in a 24-hour period:

- a reportable quantity or more of a substance listed on the CERCLA hazardous substance list
- one pound or more of a substance listed on the SARA Title III Extremely Hazardous
- Substance List (unless the release resulted in exposure only to persons within the site boundaries where the spill occurred)
- any quantity of a RCRA hazardous waste released from a tank system to the environment
- any quantity of an RCRA hazardous waste released that could threaten human health or the environment
- any release of oil to waters of the United States that causes a film or sheen on or discoloration of the surface of the water or adjoining shorelines or causes a sludge or emulsion to be deposited beneath the surface of the water or upon adjoining shorelines
- a PCB leak or release into the environment.

The CERCLA and EHS lists should be readily available at the facility. These lists are also printed in 40 CFR, 302.4 and 40 CFR, 355, Appendix A & B (EHS list).

The CERCLA list currently includes 721 hazardous substances. This list is a combination of hazardous substances identified in the following environmental laws:

- The Clean Water Act
- The Clean Air Act
- The Hazardous MAterials Transportation Act
- The Resource Conversation and recovery Act
- The Toxic Substances Control Act.

The SARA EHS list currently consists of 366 hazardous substances, 134 of which are on the CERCLA list. In order to eliminate the confusion associated with several lists, the EPA has proposed to designate the remaining 232 non-CERCLA EHSs as CERCLA hazardous substances in the near future.

Determining reportable quantities. *Reportable quantity* means, for any CERCLA hazardous substance, the reportable quantity established and identified in the CERCLA list. For extremely hazardous substances the reportable quantity is 1 Ib. RQs are typically listed in pounds.

CERCLA notification and reporting requirements are determined by identifying the chemical specific RQ and comparing it to the actual quantity of hazardous materials spilled. For each listed chemical contained in a mixture, the RQ must be determined separately by concentration and molecular weight.

The procedure for calculating RQs typically involves the following steps. An Incident Notification and Reporting Data From like the one figure must be used to record information collected as a result of these steps:

1. Identify spilled material, including individual components of mixtures. Refer to Material Safety Data Sheets for percent of hazardous ingredients. list each hazardous ingredient and its respective percentage of the mixture.

2. Match materials and their components to the RQs on the CERCLA list. List the final RQ for each material or hazardous ingredient beside the corresponding material or hazardous ingredient identified in step 1.

3. Estimate total quantity of material that was spilled. Use gallons for liquid spills, cubic feet for gases, and pounds for dry solids. For mixtures, multiply the total quantity spilled by the actual percentage for each chemical that occurs in the mixture. (total number of gallons spilled) x = Number of gallons spilled of each chemical in the mixture.

4. If the spilled material is a liquid, covert gallons to pounds by using the specific gravity for that particular chemical. (Number of gallons spilled) x (Specific gravity) x (8.3 Ib/gal) = Pounds spilled.

5. If the spilled material is a gas, convert cubic feet to pounds by using the gas density, in Ib/ft ^{3}, for that particular chemical. The specific gravity or gas density is usually specified on the MSDS. If not, refer to a chemical dictionary or call the chemical manufacturer for more information.

6. Compare results with final RQs to determine whether the spill is reportable.

The flowchart in illustrates these steps and assists response personnel during the RQ evaluation process.

Spill response management procedures

The information presented in this section can be used as a general guide in preparing facility-specific plans and procedures. Each plan and subsequent procedures will vary depending on location, conditions, and material spilled.

The EC or EPT leader may determine the need for outside assistance at any time following the discovery of a spill or after completing the spill assessment procedure. Outside services include the local fire and police departments as well as vendors that specialize in spill cleanup and disposal. The decision is based on either finding there is an imminent threat to human health or the environment, or the facility does not have sufficient personnel or adequate equipment to control the spill effectively. The dispatcher will make appropriate notification as directed by the EC.

Isolate the area. The spill site should be isolated from operational personnel to reduce the potential for exposure to hazardous substances. Scaffolds or caution ribbon may be placed around the spill site to prevent access. Remove all other hazards, if possible, including:

- electrical hazards
- incompatible chemicals or wastes

- physical hazards
- sources of ignition.

Personnel protection during spill cleanup. The following rules are aimed at reducing the potential for employee exposure to hazards during spill control and cleanup:

- Always wear personal protection to handle spilled materials. A preexisting health and safety plan should specify appropriate equipment to be worn during spill response.
- Provide medical attention as needed for personnel who have come in contact with spilled materials. Limit the number of personnel responding to the spill. Allows no unauthorized person to enter the cleanup area.
- Use the buddy system. Two people should conduct the cleanup, using line-of-sight contact with those supervising the activity.

Spill cleanup and control. This discussion provides guidance for the cleanup and control of liquids, solids, and gases.

Liquid. Stop the movement of liquid with a dike of inter absorbent material, such as vermiculite or quick-dry, and cover the remaining liquid with adsorbent.

Solvent product of waste solvent must not be allowed to flow into shop floor drains. In the event of a spill near the floor drain, cover the drain or place a dike around drain with an inert absorbent material.

Spilled oil should be collected in drums and transferred to the used oil tank. Vermiculite, quick-dry, or a similar product should be used to absorb oil residues remaining on soils or pavement.

Spilled acids and bases should be collected and transferred to the acid wastewater tank. Equipment should be used that is not reactive with the material spilled. For the remaining acid liquids, add sodium bicarbonate and work with a shovel in a circular motion a slurry. Neutralization is achieved when no bubbling is observed after addition of sodium bicarbonate. Use small amounts of dilute hydrochloric acid to neutralize basic residues.

For all liquids, use plastic scoops or shovels to transfer saturated absorbent to the proper waste containers.

Liquids should always be put in compatible containers. a tanker truck may be required for large spills.

Dry materials. Personnel should cover the spill with a trap or plastic sheet to prevent the material from blowing away before it is contained.

Small spills of dry material should be swept up and placed in a container for disposal. Large quantities of dry material should be pushed in a pile with a front-end loader and placed into drums or trucks.

Solids and sludges should be placed in drums, plastic bags, or other suitable containers. Trucks may be required for large spills.

Area contamination. Mop the spill area with water, collecting rinse water in properly labeled waste containers. Make sure that the spill site has been completely cleaned and approved for reentry before unprotected personnel are allowed to enter or resume work in the area.

Gases. Releases involving gases include acid and nitrogen fumes. When a significant quantity of gas is released, personnel should be evacuated and local emergency services contacted to control the situation.

Waste disposal. Appropriate procedures must be followed to properly characterize and manage wastes resulting from spill cleanups. Properly label and close all waste containers associated with the spill.

Contaminated soils should be excavated and characterized to determine whether they are hazardous wastes or exhibit hazardous characteristics. Even if the soil is saturated with oil, it is not considered a hazardous waste unless it exhibits at least one of the minded to be nonhazardous, it may be disposed of in a municipal or industrial solid waste landfill approved to handle such wastes. A check should be made with the disposal facility as to its permit limitations on solid and "special wastes".

Soils contaminated with solvents must be handled and disposed of a s hazardous wastes. Soils contaminate with gasoline may be aerated to remove the volatile fraction and may subsequently be disposed of in a municipal or industrial solid waste landfill.

This is usually conducted on a case-by-case basis in conjunction with state agency approval. A land application or treatment permit is usually required of a contaminated solid waste. Air quality permits may be required by state and local agencies to aerate large quantities of contaminated soil.

Follow-up activities. A facility's assessment procedures should include the actions that must be taken after the spill is under control. The procedures include consideration of the following questions during a debriefing:

- Why did the spill occur?
- What can be done to prevent reoccurrence?
- What reports must be submitted internally or to local, state, or federal agencies?
- What facility repairs or equipment replacement is required?

Remedy the cause of spill. Identify what caused the spill. Modify work practices or make necessary repairs. Typical causes of spills include.

- leaking containers
- careless transfer of product
- faulty tank valves or corroded pipes
- eroded berm around surface impoundments or containment areas resulting in overflows to nearby ditch.

Give special attention to the potential spill sources during routine site inspections to ensure that preventative and corrective measures have been implemented. Report discrepancies to the EC.

Documentation. A Spill Response Form, a sample of which appears in figure should be completed following the control of the spill. This report is useful for tracking environmental problems because it documents the circumstances surrounding the spill and the response action taken.

Emergency planning and community right-to-know

The amendments to CERCLA, know as the Superfund Amendments and Reauthorization ACt, require owners/operators of facilities to be able to respond in emergency situations. Title II of this act specifically identifies procedures or reporting hazardous substance use and spills to the community.

Section 302 of SARA required facilities that handle any of the extremely hazardous substances more than the threshold planning quantity to inform state and local officials by May 17, 1987; they must also participate in preparation of community contingency plans for hazardous materials accidents. By September 17, 1987, facilities were required to tell the local committee the name of a designated "facility emergency coordinator" who will work with the local committee in developing emergency plans. These plans were required by October 17, 1988.

The emergency release reporting requirements pursuant to Section 304 of SARA require emergency release notification of leaks, spills, and other releases of specified chemicals into the environment. Under CERCLA, those in charge of a facility, including transporters, must report to the National Response Center any spill of a specified hazardous substance in an amount equal to or greater than the RQ specified by U.S. EPA. SARA 304 significantly expands these requirements to require reporting of release of EHS chemical or CERCLA hazardous chemicals. SARA Title III requires releases to be reported immediately to the state commission and local committee and the National Response Center.

Section 311 of SARA requires facilities that must prepare or have available MSDSs for a "hazardous chemical" under OSHA to submit these MSDSs to the state commission, the local emergency planning committee, and the local fire department. Alternatively, a company may submit a list of hazardous chemicals for which it maintains MSDSs. Reporting is required for a chemical when present in excess of 10,000 Ib for OSHA hazardous chemicals, and 500Ib on the threshold planning quantity for substances on SARA's EHS list. Known as a Tier 1 Report, this form must be provided annually and contains information on the quantity and location of these hazardous chemicals at the facility aggregated by categories of physical and health hazards. The Hazardous Chemical Inventory Reporting Requirements.

Under SARA Title II, Section 313, certain facilities that manufacture, import, process, or otherwise use a chemical listed on the toxic release inventory must annually report the amount released to the environment. The first toxic chemical inventory report was due July 1, 1988, for calendar year 1987. Reports have been due annually thereafter on July 1. Facilities required to submit this report are those that (1) have 10 or more full-time employees; (2) are in standard Industrial Clarification Code 20-39; and (3) manufactured, processed, or used any of the chemicals in excess of the threshold quantity during the preceding calendar year. The U.S. EPA established phased-in threshold quantities for Section 313 reporting. For manufacturers and processors, the reporting requirement is trigged by the annual amount of a chemical: 75,000 Ib per year for 1987, 50,000 Ib per year for 19088, and 25,000 Ib per year for 1989 and thereafter. For users, reporting is triggered by use of 10,000 Ib of a chemical per year. A summary of the SARA Title III reporting requirements is provided.

Public access to facility information

Title III also requires that facilities provide the public with information about hazardous chemicals in their communities. The state commission and local committee are each required to designate an official to serve as coordinator of information. Facility coordinators must respond to requests for information form state agencies, local officials, the public, and other interested parties.

Section 324 of SARA requires that the following information be made available to the public:

- Toxic Chemical Release Inventory Reporting Forms
- MSDAs of hazardous chemicals
- Emergency and Hazardous Chemical Inventory forms
- Follow—up Emergency Notification Reports
- Local emergency response plan.

Penalties

SARA Title III contains penalties for the violation of its provisions. Civil and administration penalties include fines for companies ranging form $10,000 to as high as $75,000 for repeated violations. Violations subject to fines include the failure of a facility to:

- notify the government that it has extremely hazardous substances on-site above threshold quantities
- provide timely notification of the release of a regulated substance to the environment
- provide hazardous chemical inventory information
- provide the required Toxic Chemical Release Inventory Reporting Forms.

Criminal penalties for the knowing and willful violation of the provisions of SARA Title III can include fines and imprisonment, or both.

Medical wastes

After repeated episodes of needles, syringes, and

other medical paraphernalia appearing on U.S. beaches, Congress passed the Medical Waste Tracking Act of 1988. The MWTA charges the EPa to find an effective means of ensuring that regulated medical waste proceeds from the point of generation to an acceptable point of disposal.

Regulated medical waste is defined as waste that is capable of causing disease in humans and that may pose a risk to individual and/or community health if not treated properly. RMW consists of the following classes, ad defined in 40 CFR 22 and 259, *Standards for the Tracking and Management of MEdical Wastes* :

- *Class 1.* Cultures, Stocks and Vaccines- Class 1 includes cultures and stocks of infectious agents and associated biologics. This consists of cultures from medical laboratories, discarded live and attenuated vacccines, culture dishes, and devices used to transfer, inoculate, and mix cultures.
- *Class 2.* Pathological Waste-Class 2 medical wastes consists of human pathological wastes, including tissues, organs, or body fluids that are removed during surgery, autopsy, or other medical procedures. Also included are specimens and body fluids.
- *Class 3.* Blood and Blood Products-Class 3 wastes consist of free-flowing human blood, plasma, serum, and other blood derivatives that are waste, such as blood in blood derivatives that are waste, such as blood in blood bags or bloody drainage in suction

containers. Class 3 wastes also include items, such as gauze or bandages, that are saturated or dripping with human blood. Class 3 waste included items produced during dental procedures.

- *Class 4 and Class 7.* All Used and Unused Sharps Sharps that have been used in animal or human patient care, including hypodermic needles, syringes with or without the needle attached, Pasteur pipettes, scalpel blades, blood collection tubes and vials, test tubes, needles attached to tubing, and culture dishes are ll RMW of Classes 4 and 7. Other types of broken or unbroken glass-were that were in contact with infectious agents, such as used slides and cover slips are also included in this category.
- Call 5 is animal waste and Class 6 is isolation waste.

At the present time, medical waste is regulated in a few states under a demonstration program established by the EPA. These requirements are being followed by almost all states at the present time in anticipation of EPA's promulgating medical waste standards for all states. EPA's Report to Congress, "Medical Waste Management in the U.S." states it is EPA's intention to require the standards in 40 CFR 259 for all states, in addition to other requirements. The other requirements mentioned include new source performance standards for medical waste incinerators under the Clear Air Act, use of Best

Available Control Technology, and development by the facility operatoı of a site-specific program to handle medical waste.

In order to comply with EPA regulations for "Standards for the Tracking and Management of Medical Waste", several important factors must be analyzed:

- Is the generator employing on-site or off-site disposal of its RMW ?
- What is the monthly quantity of waste generated at the site?
- If on-site disposal is contemplated, will the RMW be commingled with either municipal waste or other regulated hazardous waste?

On-site versus off-site disposal options. Off-site disposal requires that stringent pretransportation and transpiration guidelines be followed. On-site treatment and disposal options include autoclaving or incineration. Autoclaving is relatively inexpensive and quick; however, autoclaving does not reduce the total volume of the waste. The advantage of incineration is that the volume of waste is reduced by approximately 90% . However, in order to incinerate RMW in accordance with U.S. EPA regulations, several concerns must be addressed:

- EPA regulations require stringent time and temperature standards for medical waste incineration. In particular, EPA Infectious Waste Guidelines suggest a two-second swell time at extreme temperatures. To obtain this type of performance generally requires the implementation of costly incinerators-design additions to older existing facilities. Generally, incinerators that are suitable for non hazardous municipal solid waste do not meet the time and temperature standards set forth by the EPA for biomedical waste incineration.

- Air emissions must be strictly controlled using best available emissions must be strictly. Again, incinerators that are appropriate for municipal waste disposal usually are not equipped with the required air emission control devices. Additionally, air emission permits are required for the operations of an incinerator that handles RMW.
- Fly-ash and incinerator bottom ash must be toxicity tested for hazardous waste determination.

The ash is generally considered hazardous waste unless proven otherwise.

As a result of this, it becomes essential for RMW to be segregated from non hazardous waste at the point of generation and incinerator.

Hospitals commonly use a combination of both aoutclaving and incineration. Autoclaving in itself is relatively inexpensive and renders the waste nonhazardous. Autoclaving prior to incineration alleviates the need for a biomedical classified incinerator. Additionally, an air emission permit for medical waste incineration and toxicity testing, and the potential for hazardous waste disposal of the fly-ash and bed-ash would not be necessary if the RMW was autoclaved prior to incineration. In general EPA has significantly demphasized the use of incineration technology.

Quantity of waste generated. The EPA has established "small-quantity generator" exemptions from some of the requirements for disposal of RMW for facilities that generate less than 50 Ib per month.

Mixing regulated medical waste with other waste streams. Segregating RMW from unregulated medical and nonhazrdous and hazardous wastes is essential to cost-effective RMW disposal. General non-hazardous waste that is mixed with RMW is regulated as medical waste. If RMW is incinerated with nonhazrdous waste, all of the fly-ash and bed-ash must be treated as ash generated from the incineration of RMW; that is, it must all be toxicity tested and possibly treated as hazardous waste. Additionally, if RMW is mixed with other hazardous waste that falls under the small-quantity exemption, the waste mixture must be handled and disposed as RMW under this program.

Radioactive wastes

Worldwide, the scrutiny of the proper treatment, storage, and disposal of radioactive wastes has dramatically increased since the end of the Cold War. In the United States, the U.S. DEpartment of Energy has redirected substantial funding and human resources away from bomb production and toward environmental restoration and waste management. Similar efforts are ongoing in other major nuclear countries as public opinion has focused on the nuclear waste legacy the Cold War.

Historically, U.S. definitions and requirements for permanent disposal of different classes of radioactive waste were based on the source of the waste and requirements for safe handling and storage rather than requirements for permanent disposal. This section is based on an excellent review by Kocher of the historical, legal, and regulatory requirements associated with the classification and disposal of radioactive wastes. In the United States, the regulation of radioactive wastes involves the overlapping authority of three agencies- Department of Energy, Nuclear Regulatory Commission; and Environmental Protection Agency. Thus, the reader must consult the most current directives and orders from the frequently changed regulatory guidelines and requirements.

The section presents basic information on definitions of principal classes of radioactive waste, framework of the disposal requirements for the principal waste classes, management and disposal of other radioactive wastes, and decontamination and decommissiong of existing facilities. finally, an example of the permitting and licensing requirements for a low-level mixed waste facility is included in case studies. This example illustrates the complexity and difficult of storing and disposing radioactive wastes.

Definitions of principal classes of radioactive waste

The principal classes and definitions of rad waste are:

- *Spent Fuel*: Nonreprocessed, irradiated nuclear fuel.

- *High-level wastes:* Primary waste produced from the chemical reprocessing of spent fuel.
- *Transuranic waste*: Waste that contains more than 100 nCi/g of a long-lived alpha-emitting transuranium radionuclides. High-level waste is not in this category and is separately defined. One curie is equal to the activity of 1 g of radium-226. A nanocurie is 10^{-9} ci.
- *Low-Level waste*: Waste that is not spent fuel, high-level, or uranium or thorium mill tailings. Transuranic waste is excluded from this category.

As discussed by Kocher, these definitions are generally not quantitative and do not unambiguously distinguish between the different types of waste. Therefore, under these definitions, it is possible to place rad wastes in different categories despite close similarity in properties. alternative waste classification schemes have been proposed that attempt to limit or remove ambiguities by increasing the emphasis on quantitative classification based on consideration of risks from waste disposal.

The responsibility for regulating the previously discussed rad wastes is shared by EPA, NRC, and DOE.

The EPA establishes the general environmental protection and disposal standards applicable to specified classes of civilian and defense rad waste. The standards for a particular waste class also apply to a given disposal system. EMP standards are enforced by NRC or DOE.

The NRC establishes the licensing criteria for uses and particular disposal systems regardless of rad waste class. The NRC's licensing authority covers all facilities for disposal of civilian waste and certain DOE facilities, e.g., geologic repository for civilian or defense spent fuel and high-level waste. The NRC also regulates/permits commercial nuclear power plants.

The DOE regulates disposal of defense waste that is not subject to NRC licensing, e.g., low-level waste at DOE sites.

Obviously, there are significant overlaps between the three agencies. In addition, the NRC licensing criteria are in exact opposition to the philosophic thrust of EPA standards, EPA standards are directed toward specific classes of rad waste, whereas NRC licenses particular disposal systems for any rad waste class. This decoupling of waste definition from a specific disposal requirement has one benefit: waste disposal requirements are not affected by the current problems afflicting the classification schemes.

Currently, there are only specific types of disposal systems that are authorized for disposal of some waste classes:

- geologic repository for civilian spent fuel and high-level waste and defense high-level wastes.
- waste Isolation pilot plant facility, authorized for both defense transuranic and low-level wastes.

There are no authorized intermediate disposal facilities for either dilute high-level waste, transuranic waste, or greater-than-class C low-level waste. Class C waste is an NRC definition based on radionuclide half-lives and concentrations. NRC uses this classification for near-surface land disposal. An intermediate disposal system would be a specifically designed facility located a few tens of meters below ground surface.

Management and disposal of other radioactive wastes

Other significant types of rad waste are:

- uranium of thorium or thorium mill tailings
- naturally occurring and accelerator-produced radioactive materials
- mixed waste (radioactive and hazardous chemical wastes).

Mill tailings. Mill tailings were originally regulated under the Atomic Energy Act of 1954 and are not considered a form of low-level waste under current law. The management of the tailings is governed by the Uranium Mill Tailings Radiation Control Act of 1978, also known as UMTRA. UMTRA specifically deals with the control and stabilization of mill tailings in place. If removal of railings is required because of public health or environmental concerns, permanent disposal and stabilization at non-low-level waste facilities are required. The EPA recently published updated regulations on uranium mill tailings standards, including closure.

5 Water: Softening and Mineralisation

Definitions

The calcium and magnesium content determines the hardness of water. The concentration of these ions is expressed in one of the following ways:

French degrees	**10 ppm $CaCo_3$**
German degrees	**10 ppm CaO**
British definition	**10 ppm $Ca(OH)_2$**
ppm hardness	**1ppm $CaCo_3$: (0.0648 g) per gallon (4543 L) = 14 ppm**
U.S. units	**14.26 ppm $CaCO_3$: (o.0648 g) per cubic foot (28.317 L) = 2.29 ppm**

These expressions are based on an equivalent amount a calcium carbonate even when the compounds present are not calcium salts but magnesium salts. For example, 10 ppm $Mg(HCO_3)_2$ represents 0.0685 mM or 0.137 mEq/L Mg_2+. Then the equivalent of calcium concentration is also 0.17 mEq/L or 6.85 ppm $CaCO_3$ or 0.685 Fr. hardness.

Temporary hardness is due to bicarbonates or carbonates only, while permanent hardness also implies ions other than those from carbonic acid (e.g., sulfates and chlorides).

Importance of mineralization of drinking water

Drinking water is considered to be consumed at 2 to 2.5 L/day per person. The calcium needs per day per person range from 600 to 1000 mg. Of this total, 200 mg/day is taken in directly as calcium ion through the intestine. The contribution from drinking water can range between 10mg/L (25 ppm $Caco_3$ hardness) and 120 ppm (300 ppm $CaCO_3$ hardness) (1, ranging from marginal to complete needs. Also, evidence has been produced that calcium is probably less well absorbed from water than from other foodstuffs.

The daily need for magnesium ranges from 300 to 500 mg. Standard contents in foodstuffs are much lower than for calcium; examples (in mg per 100 g food) are cheese, 40; milk, 11; fish, 25; eggs, 11;vegetables, 20; and meat, 25. This means that the contribution to the magnesium needs provided by water is significant, and moreover, it appears that the magnesium ion is well absorbed. Therefore, if drinking water is softened, the process should maintain the magnesium concentration high enough to contribute to the average daily intake of this significant element.

The intake of increased amounts of sodium has been analyzed critically in relation to the risk of increased blood pressure. In a normal food regime daily intake as NaCl is considered as 3 g/day, the normal food intake brings about 3.5 g Na/day. A strongly restricted diet represents a daily intake of 0.9 g na. In Europe, the maximum admitted concentration of sodium in drinking water is 150 mg/L. The exchange of 300 ppm

$CaCO_3$ can introduce 138 mg/L sodium; hence care must be taken not to exceed the maximum allowable concentration.

Potential advantages of softening

Problems such as corrosion and bacterial development often occur with water softeners installed in private houses. These are due to lack or maintenance and could be avoided or lessened if the softening were centralized by the water authority. Italy has established legally binding conditions for the household treatment of water.

Calcium and magnesium salts of soaps (e.g., fatty acids) are nearly insoluble in water, so precipitation of these salts, particularly on textiles, may occur during washing. The problem is less important when synthetic detergents are used.

Scale formation in boilers is another drawback of hard water. The bicarbonate ion decomposes as the temperature rise and forms carbonates:

$$2HCO_3^- \rightarrow CO_3^{2-} = H_2O = CO_2$$

Since the carbonate of calcium is only slightly soluble, precipitation occurs:

$$Ca^{2+} + CO_3^{2-} \rightarrow CaCO_3\downarrow$$

If large amounts of magnesium are also present, insoluble magnesium hydroxide can be precipitated:

$$Mg_2 + 2OH^- \rightarrow Mg(OH)_2 = MgO + H_2O$$

If present, other anions can also precipitate

(e.g., calcium and magnesium silicates, which are almost insoluble):

$$Ca^{2+} + SiO_3^{2} \rightarrow Casio_3$$

$$Mg^{2+} + SiO_3^{2-} \rightarrow MgSiO_3$$

The normal flow of the water is hindered by clogging of the pipes due to these scale deposits, while hear conduction in boilers is also reduced. Water containing a total hardness of 1 mEq $CaCO_3$/L is considered "soft"; while a content above 5 mEq/L is called "hard water."

Certain secondary benefits of lime softening are:

1. A bactericidal effect, due to the high pH reached in some processes
2. Elimination of iron, particularly the ferrous form found in well waters
3. Partial elimination of organic products, by coprecipitation
4. Reduction in concentrations of trace elements, such as Hg, Pb, and Zn, by incorporation in the crystals when crystallization method is used

The softening of drinking water is unnecessary from a hygienic point of view; soft waters are even suspected to promote cardiovascular diseases. However, for most uses, hard water is less desirable, specifically for laundering.

Calcium carbonate equilibria

Waters oversaturated with calcium carbonate tend to precipitate $CaCO_3$; when undersaturated, they tend to dissolve calcium carbonate and are, eventually, corrosive. There exist numerous indexes and graphical methods of evaluating the equilibrium conditions versus $CaCO_3$. Only a few of the fundamentals are outlined here.

The total concentration of carbonic species present in water involves carbonic acid (or dissolved carbon dioxide), bicarbonate, and carbonate: H_2CO_3 HCO_3^-, and CO_3^{2-}, respectively. The concentrations of these species are interrelated by equilibrium reactions:

$$H_2CO_3 \rightleftharpoons H^+ + HCO_3^-$$

$$K_1 = \frac{[H^+][HCO_3^-]}{[H_2CO_3]}$$

$$HCO_3^- \rightleftharpoons H^+ + CO_3^{2-}$$

$$K_2 = \frac{[H^+][CO_3^{2-}]}{[HCO_3^-]}$$

$$K_1 = 4.07 \times 10^{-7} \quad pK_1 = 6.39 \quad (20°C)$$

$$K_2 = 4.17 \times 10^{-11} \quad pK_2 = 10.38 \quad (20°C)$$

Effect of ionic strength

The above-mentioned "thermodynamic" equilibrium constants are values applicable at infinite dilutions of a single salt. To account for real conditions a correction for the ionic strength of the water needs to be used. Operational equilibrium constants can be deduced from he thermodynamic constants by introducing an appropriate factor for correction of the salt content of the water, called the ionic strength factor. The ionic strength is equal to

$$\mu = \tfrac{1}{2}(\Sigma\, C_1 V_1^2 + \Sigma\, C_2 V_2^2)$$

in which $V_1 = 1$, $V_2 = 2$, and C_2 and C_2 are the respective concentrations (ion g/L) of mono- and divalent ions in water. if a fully worked-out ionic balance for the water is not available, reasonable approximations are given by in which H is the total hardness in moles per liter and A the alkalinity in equivalents per liter.

$$\mu = 4H - A$$

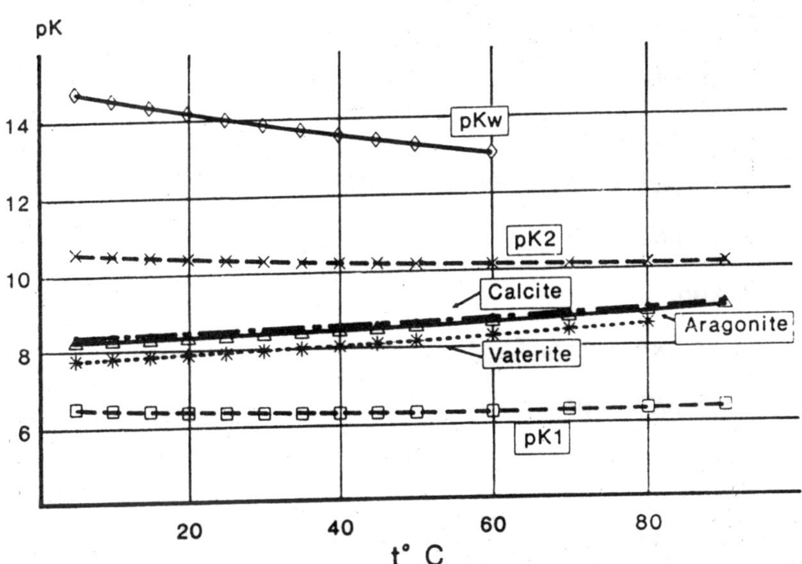

Graphical correlation of the effect of temperature on ***calcium*** *carbonate equilibria*

The ionic strength of the solution determines an approximate activity factor of each ion:

$$-\log f = 0.5V^2\sqrt{\mu} \quad (\text{e.g., } V = 2;\ -\log f = 2\sqrt{\mu})$$

The operational equilibrium constants K° are obtained by correcting the equilibrium constants for an activity factor:

$$K_S^\circ = f_{Ca}[Ca^{2+}]\,f_{CO_3}[CO_3^{2-}] = K_S = [Ca^{2+}][CO_3^{2-}]$$

Hence

$$K_S^\circ = K_S f_{Ca^{2+}} f_{CO_3^{2-}}$$

$$pK_S^\circ = pK_S - \log f_{Ca^{2+}} - \log f_{CO_3^{2-}} = pK_S - 2\sqrt{\mu} - 2\sqrt{\mu}$$

$$pK_S^\circ = pK_S - 4\sqrt{\mu}$$

Similarly,

$$K_w^\circ = Kf_{H^+}f_{OH^-}$$

$$K_w^\circ = pK_w - \log f_{OH^-} = pK_w - 0.5\sqrt{\mu} - 0.5\sqrt{\mu}$$

$$pK_w^\circ = pK - \sqrt{\mu}$$

Also,

$$K_1^\circ = K_1 f_{H^+} f_{HCO_3^{2-}}$$

$$pK_1^\circ = pK_1 - \sqrt{\mu}$$

And

$$K_2^\circ = K_2 = \frac{f_{H^+}f_{CO_3^{2-}}}{f_{HCO_3^-}} = K_2 f_{CO_3^{2-}}$$

$$pK_2^\circ = pK_2 - 2\sqrt{\mu}$$

Calculation of the *pHs* value is corrected by taking as a basis the difference in the equilibrium constants corresponding to the operational constants of K_2 and K_s. Consequently,

$$pH_S = (pK_2^\circ - pK_S^\circ) + pCa + pAlk$$

Effects of heterogeneity

The equilibrium constants given above are related to homogeneous solutions of ions. However, when precipitation or dissolution of hardness is concerned, the system is heterogeneous and solid-liquid contact must be considered. An approach has been published that can be handled on the basis of the equilibrium constants.

Immersed solid $\Leftrightarrow K_s^*$ equilibrated solid

particle size of *d* - molar size *d*

molar size - molecular surface *s*

An approximation is for the relationship between particle size and molecular surface. Suppose that 1 mol of finely powdered solid consists of N uniform particles of equal size. Than the surface of a single particle corresponds to S = kd^2 and the volume is V = ld^2. The molar volume is V = M/p and

$$\overset{\circ}{s} = NS = \frac{N\alpha V}{d} = \frac{M\alpha}{\rho d}$$

where = K/l is the empirical shape factor of the particles (=1 if perfect spheres); or, the diameter/length ratio in cylinders, p the density of the solid, M the formula molar weight of the solid, and the mean Gibbs energy of the solid-liquid interface.

$$\Delta G = -RT \ln K_{S,o} \pm 2RT \ln 55 = \tfrac{2}{3}\bar{\gamma}$$

$$= \frac{2M}{3}\frac{\alpha\bar{\gamma}}{d} = RT \ln \frac{K_S(s,d)}{K_S(s = 0;\ d = \infty)}$$

The equations become

$$\log K_S^* \text{ (immersed solid)} = \log K_{S,o}^*(d = \infty) + \frac{0.2895M\alpha\bar{\gamma}}{RT}\, d^{-1}$$

$$\log K_S^* \text{ (equilibrated solid)} = \log K_{S,o}^*(s = 0) + \frac{0.2895\bar{\gamma}}{RT}\, s$$

Caustic soda process

Caustic soda is easier to handle than are lime and soda ash. The use of sodium hydroxide must be considered on a comparative economic basis. Sodium hydroxide precipitates both carbonate and noncarbonate hardness, and there is less sludge than with lime. Below 6°C the reaction velocity with lime decreases strongly, while that with caustic soda is quite independent of temperatures between 1 and 22°C. The global environmental impact is in favor of lime since sodium hydroxide usually results from synthetic procedures which also deliver residues.

Softening with sodium phosphate

When reacting with calcium and magnesium ions, sodium phosphate produces insoluble phosphates; for example:

$$3Ca(HCO_3)_2 + 2Na_3PO_4 \rightarrow Ca_3(PO_4)_2 + 6NaHCO_3$$

$$3CaSO_4 + 2Na_3PO_4 \rightarrow Ca_3(PO_4)_2 + 3Na_2SO_4$$

Technical ex·-:ution of lime softening

Precipitation

The softening process may be carried out in conventional flocculator-[clarifiers, but usually the operation is performed at higher surface loadings. A rapid-mixing basin is necessary and 5 to 10 min is sufficient for the residence time in the mixing zone. Floc growth and precipitation take place within 40 to 60 min. Since the process is facilitated by contact with particularly well suited to the backmixing concept. Classical surface loading is kept under 5 m/h. In horizontal flow-sedimentation basins used in lime softening, the retention time should be between 2 and 4 h, with a horizontal flow of 18 m/h. The sludge is drawn off as a 5 to 15% slurry. Scrapers are used to facilitate sludge removal.

Crystallization

The calcium carbonate formed in the softening process can be precipitated either as flocs or as crystals. The formation of these crystals is promoted by crystallization nuclei of calcium carbonate. Classically, the dimensions of the inoculation grains are between 0.2 and 1 mm. it is essential that the grains remain in suspension and do not grow together to from a solid mass. This process proceeds much faster than floc growth, so that surface loadings of 50 to 100 m/h are possible. The method eliminates primarily the calcium hardness, but some magnesium is also removed as $CaMg(CO_3)_2$ and $CaCO_3$ $MgCO_3$ built in the calcium carbonate crystallization lattice. The Gyractor is a typical from of traditional commercial equipment used in the crystallization technique. The total height of the apparatus can attain 5 m, with a crystallization zone of about 2 m.

Much recent progress has been made in the technology of crystallization as a result of research and applications in the Netherlands. From this research the following facts are now known, which can determine new progress:

1. The rate of softening can be very high; crystallization on nucleation material occurs within seconds.
2. Well-calibrated sand is necessary as nucleation material, starting from 0.1 to 0.3 mm and growing to 0.2 to 0.6 mm. At the size of 0.4 to 0.6 mm on crystallization, they need to be removed to prevent clogging. These guide values depend also on the surface loading.

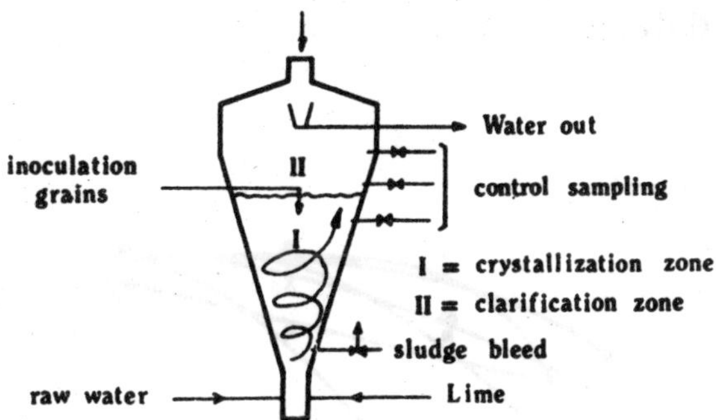

Schematic of the Gyractor crystallizator

Secondary benefits of chemical softening

Removal of heavy metals

A large number of heavy metals can be removed or lowered in concentration due to the reduction in solubility of their oxyanions, including hydroxy carbonates at increasing pH. This is the case, for example, for Zn, Ni, Cu, Co, Cd, Hg, Te, Cr, Ag, Mn, and Fe. It is worth noting that to be efficient, pH values of 9 and higher must be obtained. This puts into question the necessity of maintaining a minimum magnesium content in the drinking water. Also, water with too high a pH is less well suited for cooking dough and pastalike materials.

Removal of organic compounds by chemical softening

Addition of lime has been described as increasing the removal of BOD and improving the sludge conditioning reported in earlier literature. Indicative data areillustrated. About half of the BOD, can be removed by lime precipitation. if ozone is also used, the removal rate can be 80 to

85%. However, the pH must be 10 and higher to obtain this result, which is in agreement with literature data.

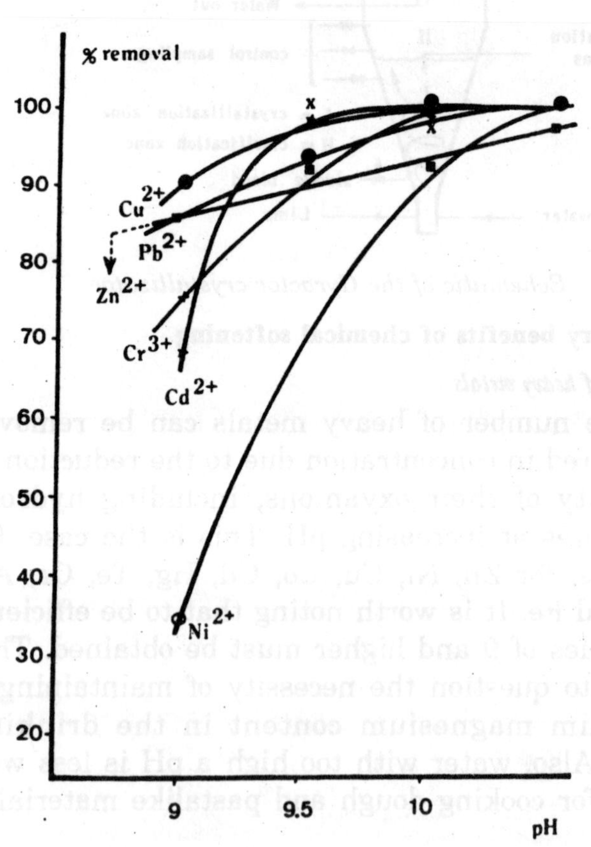

Coprecipitation of heavy metals in chemical softening

Disinfection

Excess-lime treatment of water was reported very early as a method of removal of coliforms as well as other enteric pathogens. Typical results obtained in the laboratory are illustrated. to

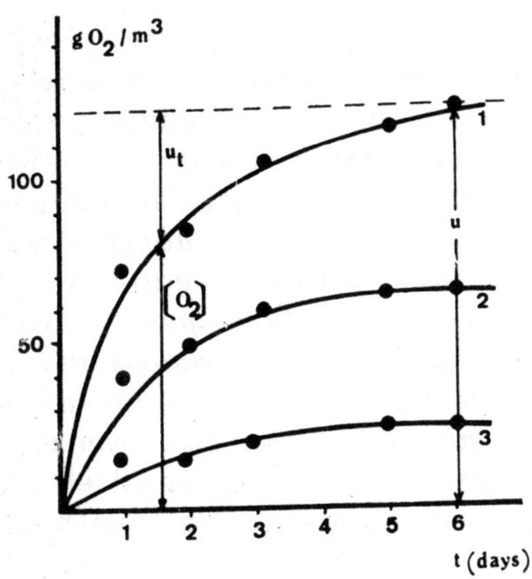

Removal of BOD from wastewater by precipitation with li,e, river Senne, Brussels

summarize: High pH values speed up the effect, but the necessary reaction time ranges up to several hours. For more ubiquitous bacteria such as wild strains of pseudomonas fluorescens, the behavior on lime treatment may be hazardous, as illustrated. In all instances high pH values and long reaction times are necessary to obtain a significant amount of decay. In conclusion: for the purpose of disinfection, excess-lime treatment is only an emergency technology for use in the absence of other disinfectants.

Water treatment by exchange

Ion exchangers

Ion exchange is defined as the reversible interchange of structural ions of materials called ion exchangers with ions in solutions contacted with the ion exchangers. General reviews have been published on the subject as applicable to water treatment. *Cationic exchangers exchange cations and thus contain negatively charged groups in their structure. Consequently, contrary to the definitions of the charge of cations and cationic polyelectrolytes, cationic resins are negatively charged cationic exchangers.* The reverse are the anionic exchangers containing positively charged groups that combine reversibly with various negative ions.

In 1833, Fuchs observed that "when certain clays are treated with lime, they release potassium." In 1848, evidence of exchange of calcium versus ammonium ions in soils was produced by Thompson and Way. The reversibility of the process was fully assessed around 1850. Manganese oxide as a nonstoichiometric compound is composed of a mixture of MnO and MnO_2 approaching the structure

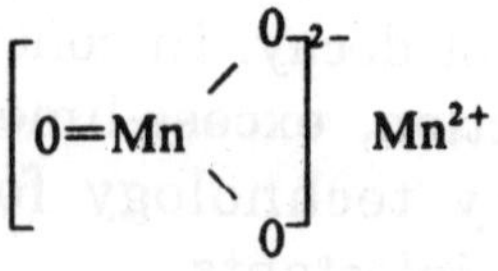

$$\left[O{=}Mn\begin{matrix} \diagup O \\ \diagdown O \end{matrix} \right]^{2-} Mn^{2+}$$

in which Mn^{2+} can be exchanged with Fe^{2+}. for example.

Around the beginning of this century ion-exchange properties were assessed for several natural minerals, including bentonite clays, glauconite (greensand), and conditioned silica gels. The first synthetic ionic exchangers were the synthetic zeolites (from the Greek zein-lithos, meaning "boiling stone"), patented in 1906. They were composed of a fused mixture of SiO_2 + $Al_2O_3(H_2O)$. Later, the product was prepared by a gelling process of silicate and aluminate, the gel later being dried and crushed to grain size. These first synthetic exchangers had very slow exchange kinetics and could eventually deteriorate by losing the silicate portion by dissolution in water.

Synthetic exchange resins

Current commercial ion exchangers are, at present, synthetic resins in which functional groups act as exchangers. Effective ionic exchangers must:

1. Contain ions in their own structure
2. Be insoluble in water under the operational conditions (temperature, acidity, basicity, etc.)
3. Have a porous structure enabling diffusion of the ions throughout the structure.

During the 1930s it was discovered that sulfonated organic products were capable of cationic exchange. At that time sulfonated phenolic resins were obtained by condensation of m-phenolsulfonic acid and formol.

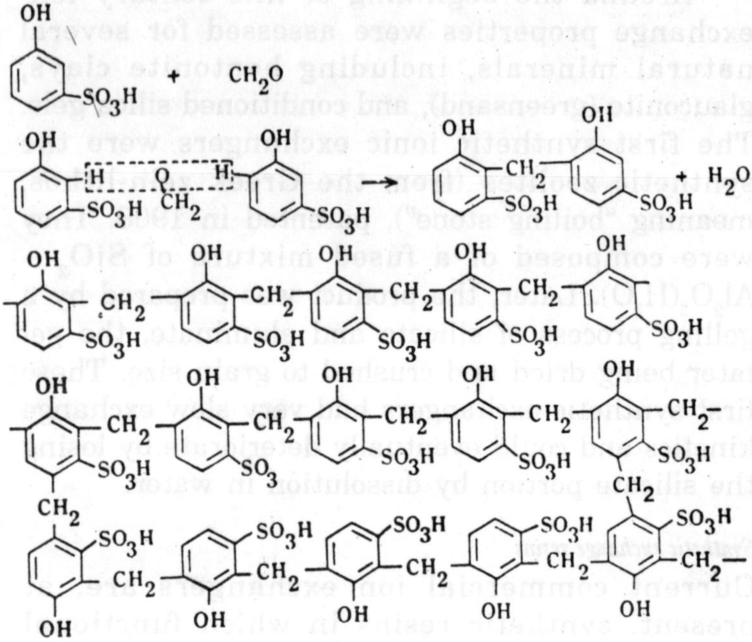

A fundamental discovery was made in 1945 by d'Alelio, who patented a sulfonated polystyrene polymer capable of cationic exchange.

Sulfonated coal and sulfonated phenolic resins deteriorate in the presence of dissolved chlorine. Obtaining and maintaining a reporducible porous structure was problem with sulfonated polystyrene homopolymers, The resins, designated here by "Res," are actually synthetic reticulated polymers, usually resulting from copoly-merization of styren and divinylbenzene.

Functional groups are substituted into the benzene rings (e.g., on sulfonation or ammonitation), thus providing the exchanger groups.

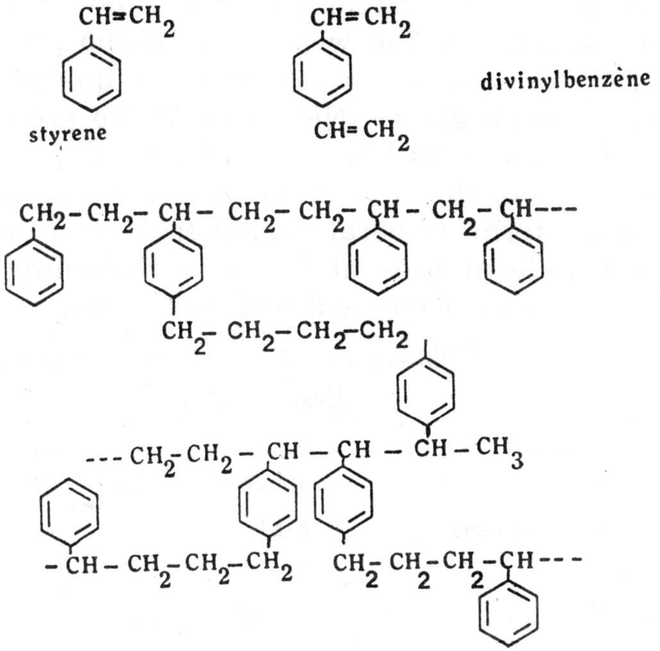

styrene

divinylbenzene

Advanced technologies of copolymerization have made it possible to improve the pore structure to obtain equally spaced cross-links determining an "isoporous structure" (i.e., a material with micropores of uniform size). In "macroporous" resins a spongelike structure is obtained with a network of tightly corsslinked molecules with intermolecular holes that are larger than the single moleculare size.

Polyacrylic resins macroporous resins can allow efficient reversible adsorption of organic material, which is a more recent development in ionic exchange. The most common functional groups for cationic exchangers are the carboxyl group (COOH) (weak acid resins) and the sulfonic group (-SO_3H) (Strong acid resins). Anionic exchangers are the weak basic imino group (-NRH_2^+/OH^-) and the strong basic quaternary ammounium group (-NR_3^+/OH^-). If the proton of the acid goups (COOH) or (-SO_3H) is replaced by a sodium ion, the resin is defined as being in its sodium form. General characteristics of resins applicable at present for water softening are given. Granulometry is determined by wet sieving.

General gharacteristics of Cation-Exchange Resins

Appearance	White to reddish-brown spheres	
% Divinylbenzene	8-14	
Density	1.3	
Liter weight	800-880 kg/m3	
Mositure content (native)	30-50 wt%	
Sieve analysis (example)	Diameter (mm)	Passing (%)
	<o.2	0.5
	0.22	3
	o.42	14
	o.62	42.2
	o.84	36.3
	1.19	4
Effective size (mm)	0.4-0.6	
Uniformity coefficient	1.5-1.8	
Viod volume	30-40 (vol %)	

Determination of total exchange capacity

The total exchange capacity is defined at 20°C and must be determined at 20 # 5°C. The determinationis achieved either by a batch technique or in a testing column containing a given volume of ion exchanger in the standard state. Preliminary hydration with pure water is the first step of test procedure. Very detailed descriptions of standard test columns are indicated in the literature, as well as mathematical models for break-through profiles.

Simplifying, the test is carried out in a column of diameter/height ratio between 1/20 and 1/15. The column is filled with wetted resin at two-thirds of its height. For resins used in the sodium form the exchanger is stabilized in the column by percolating a solution of 50 to 70 g NaCl/L and using a quantity of 0.4 kg NaCl/L of wetted resin. The column is rinsed with distilled water and must be maintained permanently wetted.

The water under investigation is passed through the column at a flow of 5 to 10 column volumes per hour. If W is the volume of the water exchanged for S (milli) equivalents per liter by an ion exchanger of volume *V* in the column, the total exchange capacity is

$$T = \frac{W \times S}{V}$$

The break-through capacity corresponds to

$$T = \frac{W \times (S \times S')}{V}$$

where S' is the average ionic content in the effluent.

Use of ion exchangers

Apart from rare cases, such as the reduction of sulfates, niitrate removal, or desalinization, total demineralizaiton of drinking water is seldom undertaken. Softening with substitution. of Ca/Mg ions by sodium ions is more frequent, partiicularly in municipal supplies, and in Europe, particularly on a household scale.

The softening process does not alter the alkalinity of the water:

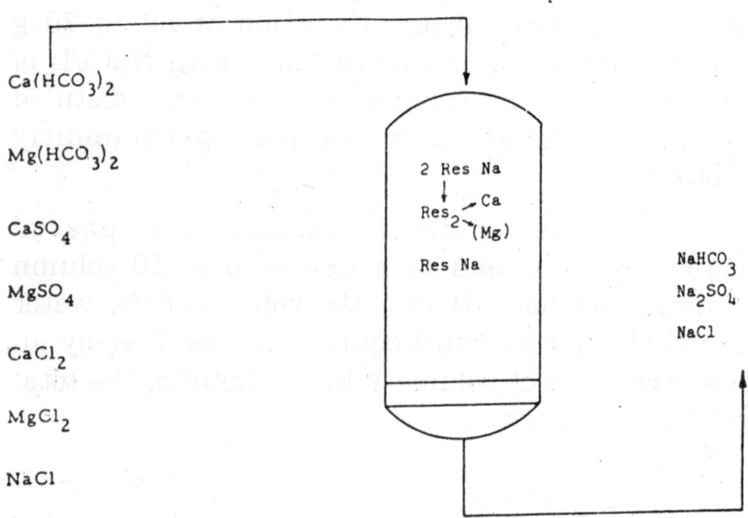

Although the process has been developed in open filters, the most common method remains the downflow pressure filter, particularly on a household scale.

In the decarbonatation process, exchangeon a ResH+ basis and using acids for regeneration, decarbonation of the water can be obtained according to the following scheme:

The neutralization of the acids H2SO4 and HCl can eventually be obtained by subsequent passage through an anion exchanger.

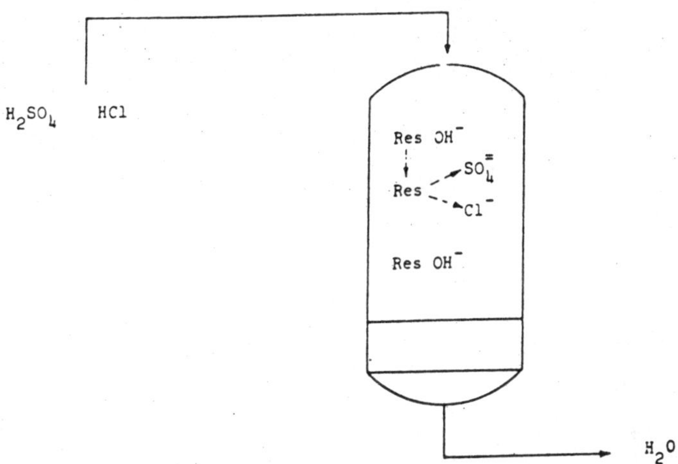

Removal of silica and CO_2

The removal of dissolved silica (silicic acids) as well as CO_2 (carbonic acid) requires strong basic or anionic resins. The application is important for waters to beused in high-pressure biolers. The same principles hold for the removal of carbonic acid. As a strong basic resin is also necessary, the latter must be regenerated with sodium hydroxide (e.g., a 4% solution). An aeration step is to be provided to dissipate most of the CO_2 and thus to spare the regeneration solution.

Use of macroporous resins

Strong basic anio-exchange resins in the chloride from can be used for the removal of humic acids. A full-scale plant is in operation at the Fuhrberg plant of the Hannover Waterworks. The best resin has a macroporous structure that is favorable for the adsorption of larger molecules. Sulfate ions interfere since owing to their hihger exchange coefficient, sulfates replace chlorides. In Fuhrgerg water, containing 130 mg/L SO_4^{2-}, a throughput of about 300 bed volumes can be reached. With the resin in the sulfate form, about 50% of the humic acids is still removed up to 5000-bed-volume transit.

Possible throughput is up to 50 bed volumes per hour (four filters of 12.5 m3 resing each), With a total cycle of 4 days between regeneration. Removal of the humic acids ranges from 85% (beginning of the filtration cycle) to 55%, with an initial dissolved organic carbon input of 6.5 mg/L. Nitrification of the dissolved nitrogen compounds sets in gradually. Elution of nitrite must be considered. Regeneration of the exchange filters is obtained by the transit of two bed volumes of a solution containing 100 g/L NaCl and 20g/L NaOH.

Operational sequences

A single-phase strong cationic resin in its sodium form is the most used technology for softening.

Regeneration is possible by passing a suitable solution downward(e.g., NaCl 25 g/L; complete regeneration may necessitate 5 mole of Ca/Mg salt exchanged); the regeneration contact time is in the range 20 to 45 min; the volume of brine is between 0.5 and 1.5 times the volume of the resin. Often a less concentrated brine solution is used (e.g., 10%). The regeneration is followed by washing with clear water. Part of this wash water can be recovered as the so-called "compound" and used subsequently in regeneration preliminary to transit of the brine solution.

Solid conditioned Nacl combined with adequate rinsing devices can be used for household applications according to the instructions of the equipment manufacturer.(e.g., washing machines). Filtered seawater can be used for regeneration, but its Ca/Mg content must be considered. The flow of the regeneration liquid must be increased accordingly.

A cationic exchanger followed by a strong basic exchanger is the simplest design of a flowsheet for complete demineralization. The exact sequence of the different exchangers must be considered as a function of the water to be treated: The classical sequence is a strong cationic exchanger-decarbonation-deaeration- a strong anionic exchanger. However, if the water is heavily charged with anions necessitating a strong anionic exchanger, the preferred sequence can become strong cationic exchanger-weak anionic exchanger-decarbonation-deaeration-strong anionic exchanger.

Also, a "top layer" of a weak acid-exchanging resin can remove the calcium-magnesium ions, and a subsequent strong acid exchanger, the remaining alkalinoter rous ions together with the neutral salts. Mixed beds can also be used: mixed anionic and cationic resins separated hydraulically for regeneration.

Guidelines for design

General data on softening with cationic exchangers are given as follows:

Exchange capacity: 700 to 1250 kg/m^3

Bed depth: 0.6 to 1 m

Softening and mineralization

Surface loading: 10 to 16 m/h (exceptionally, 50)

Backwash speed: 12 m/h

Regeneration time: 25 to 45 min

Rinse flow:

Fast 20 to 40 m/h

Slow 8 to 15 m/h

Rinse volume: 3 to 5 m^3/m^3 resin

Ion exchange can be operated with technologies similar to the ones applied in rapid sand filtration. The bed depth must be at least 0.75 m, to avoid premature break-through. Usually, it is not higher than 2 m, to avoid excessive head loss. The usual surface loading reaches 6 to 15 m/h, but higher velocities (e.g., 20 to 40 m/h) are possible. The process has the following components:

1. The fixative exchanger (e.g., ca^{2+}, Mg^{2+} retention); the velocity depends on the water flow (e.g., 5 to 10 filter volumes/h).
2. Expansion by countercurrent washing (elimination of deposits, colloidal precipitates, air pockets, or channels); an expansion of regenerating solution by a downward water flow; the volume of the rinsing solution is kept between 2.5 and 5 times the volume of the exchanger.

The entire process is best controlled automatically (e.g., by measurement of the electrical conductivity of the effluents). The surface loading of the ionic exchange filters influence both the exchange efficiency obtained and the head loss, which is also dependent of the water temperature. The exchange efficiency is largely independent of the water flow since the ion-exchange process is fast. The limits of 16 to 40 m^3/h resin are recommended to maintain steady exchange conditions.

As a conclusion, the head loss remains very low in all instances as long as in ion exchange is the slow process occurring (i.e., as long as no suspended matter is filtered by the exchanger). As the bed expansion on countercurrent regeneration is high, with considerable risk of resin loss, an indicative sequence that is generally preferred.

Design rules of ion-exchange softeners

An applicable general formula is

$$E = \frac{K \times B \times Q \times H}{G \times T}$$

Where

E = volume of the exchange material (m_3)

K = safety factor for irreversible adsorption (generally, 0.75 to 0.8).

B = break-through capacity (kg $CaCO_3.m^3$)

Q = volume of water to be treated between regeneration (m^3)

H = hardness of the raw water (kg/m^3)

G = hardness removed between two regenerations (kg/m^3)

T = total exchange capacity of the resin (kg $CaCO_3/m^3$)

Design checklist:

Water flow

Softening requirements

Time between regenerations

Layout of the units

Resin exchange capacity

Hydraulic characteristics of the resin

Underdrain and backwash system

Brine makeup and storage

In general

Layer thinckness ranger: 50 to 150 cm.

Backwash expansion: 80 to 100% of bed depth is taken into consideration.

Resin volume range of softeners: 1.5 to 120 m^3. Vertical softeners operated under pressure may have diameters up to 3.6 m (minimum 25 cm). (For household or limited used, pressure-type systems of smaller volume are available.)

Water inlet: similar to that for rapid sand filters.

Brine inlet: same as for water inlet if downflow regeneration.

Underdrain system: must be resistant to corrosion by brine and to aggressive softened waters. Homogeneous distribution of fluids must be obtained by a manifold pipe distribution system. The underdrain can be constructed on the basis of built-in strainer in a concrete floor or as a composite gravel underdrain. The minimum layer thickness is of 25 to 30 cm composed, for example, of several sizes of gravel (e.g., 10 to 15 cm 0.3 to 0.6 mm in size; completed with 10 to 15 cm of 10 to 20 mm).

Brine makeup and storage: experience has proven that the withdrawal of brine from the bottom of the storage tank with water feed at the top is the preferred dosing form. Wet storage is preferable and the brine is best made up immediately after delivery or even during unloading of the transport units themselves (boat, trucks, etc.) (for small used, continuous-flow-through units with solid conditioned tablets releasing the necessary brine on flow-through of the regneration water).

Materials

Generally, stainless steel, except for the high-titanium grades are not acceptable because of "chloride corrosion."

Suitable epoxy coatings are recommended for both steel and concrete surfaces. Suitable epoxy coatings are recommended for both steel and concrete surfaces. Foodstuff-grade plastics on the basis of PE, PTFE, PP, and PVC are recommended.

Ebonite-vitrified equipment performs well but is outside the acceptable price range.

Operational control: similar to that of rapid sand filtration except that the measurement of electrical conductivity of inlet and outlet water and of regeneration and rinsing waters is the determinant.

Problems associated with ion-exchange softening

Spent brine

Disposal of spent brine or exhausted regeneration liquids can involve considerable problems. The volume of wastewaters usually represents 3 to 4% (range 1.5 to 7) of the production capacity. Moreover, the waste brine composition may contain 35 to 100% dissolved solids. Direct uncontrolled discharge in a river may be harmful to fish life. Where dilution in a river is allowed, it must be controlled so that the preestablished level of salinity will not be exceeded. Ocean disposal of the spent brine is undoubtedly the most acceptable solution to the problem.

Precipitates

Iron, manganese, and aluminum precipitating in the resin beds can seriously affect the exchange capacity. Ferrous iron can be flushed to the waste during regeneration. A rejuvenation process is based on the reduction in situ of the ferric deposits by the use of $NaHSO_3$ in the regenerating liquid. Occasional treatment of strong cationic resins with HCL can improve resin lifetime when a problem occurs with manganese fouling. Preliminary tests or advice of the manufacturer of the resin are required to be able to use these techniques.

Aggressivity

The bicarbonate content of the water is unchanged but the calcium is eliminated; in most cases this renders the water aggressive according to Langelier:

$$I = \mathrm{pH} - \mathrm{pH}_S$$

$$\mathrm{pH}_S = (\mathrm{p}K_2 - \mathrm{p}K_S) + \mathrm{pCa} + \mathrm{pAlk}$$

The possible aggressivity of the resulting water must always be into consideration.

Sodium content

With strong cationic resins in their sodium form, in the softened water the calcium ions are exchanged for sodium ions. Although the level at which the sodium may be present is believed to be harmless, it still remains necessary to pay attention to possible effects of an increase in sodium.

Example. Several operating municipal plants have been described in the United States. In Europe, the municipal Tournai plant (Belgium) is a typical example.

Example of tournai (Belgium). Open type-filter exchangers:

Bed expansion at 6 to 12 m/h starting at high velocity and then slowing down; total time, for example, 8 min

Downflow regeneration at a speed of 2 to 3 m/h

Downflow rinsing at a speed of 5 to 10 m/h

The entire regeneration cycle can last up to 1 h, the different phases being in the range of 1 for bed expansion, 2.5 for regeneration, and 1 for rinsing.

Mineralization and stabilization of water

Starting from an equilibrated water, an aggressive water can result due to several causes:

1. Hydrolysis of aluminum sulfate, converting bicarbonate to carbon dioxide:

   $Al2(SO_4)_3 + 6HCO_3^- \longrightarrow 3SO_4^{2-} + 2Al(OH)_3 + 6CO_2$

2. Fermentation: for example, for glucose

   $C_6H_{12}O_6 + 6O_2 \longrightarrow 6CO_2 + H_2O$

3. Softening, particularly by ionic exchange in closed pressure filters, removes the calcium content but leaves the carbonic acid content unchanged

4. Treatment of water with acids for auxiliary reasons such as optimization of coagulation
5. Natural waters with low mineralization
6. Mixing of two or several waters [the Tillmans graph is not linear in correlating CO_2 versus HCO_3 - (e.g., in miming waters A and B are equal proportions, a composition C results which is aggressive); consequently, the water service must take care of the problem as a whole and compute the equilibrium of the final product]

Lime-softened waters

Lime-softened waters can require recarbonation as described above. The American Water Works Association have defined a goal standard of minimum 80 to 100 mg/ L hardness as $CaCo_3$. Most European legislations converge to a minimum required hardness of 54 to 60 mg/L calcium (135 to 150 ppm as $CaCO_3$), but also a minimum in magnesium concentration is often required [e.g., 6 mg/L (or 25 ppm as $CaCO_3$)].

The major problem associated with lime softening with or without recarbonation is post-precipitation, as has been know since the 1950s. The problem is curs. Data as reported are, for example, that waters of 24 ppm supersaturation storage. A supersaturated water of 30 ppm hardness can lose up to 15 ppm on longer storage (e.g., 15 ppm precipitated.) Moreover, if in the storage reservoirs, the water transportation mains or household equipment scale deposits exist, they can act as seeds for further precipitation of calcium carbonate. The particle size of magnesium oxide seeds plays an important role in the speed of deposition or settling; at 75µm or less, deposition occurs within minutes.

The zeta potential or electrophoretic mobility of the colloidal $CaCO_3$ or $Mg(OH)_2$-MgO particles also plays a very important role. At alkaline pH values such as those that occur in softened water, it is remarkable that calcium carbonate colloids are negatively charged, while magnesium hydroxide-oxide colloids appear to be positive. Hence the complementarity of Ca/Mg can play an important role in lime precipitation through coagulation by mutual neutralization of colloids. It is generally recommended that filtration stage be included after lime treatment.

Correction of aggressivity

Although the Langelier index cannot be correlated immediately with the quantity of potential precipitate or dissolving of material, it may generally be recommended that *I* be higher than + 0.3 and never lower than -0.2. If the water is aggressive, several corrective methods can be employed.

Aeration

The equilibrium concentration of dissolved CO_2 versus air is about 1 mg CO2/L. Consequently, by spraying the water, it is possible to diminish the amount of dissolved CO_2. The process has the advantage of making it possible to saturate the water with oxygen. In practice, by spray aeration alone, it is not possible to obtain a water containing less than 3 to 5 mg CO2/L. The equilibrium implicates an alkalinity of at least 100 to 120 ppm. The process is self-limited and does not alter the hardness of the water. Aeration is indirectly involved in the dispersal of ozonated air in water during ozonization as a final stage of treatment.

Filtration through granulated marble

The analytical determination of the aggressivity or precipitativity of a water requires equilibration versus $CaCO_3$ and subsequent determination of its change in composition. From a theoretical standpoint, filtration through marble should be a very elegant method for the correction of aggressivity: The equilibrium cannot be surpassed, and if the filters are sufficiently large, changes in the carbon dioxide content of the raw water do not necessitate direct adjustment. The precipitation of iron and manganese on the marble grains is inherent in the process and thus inactivated the material. Consequently, backwashing becomes necessary.

The operation can be carried out in open and closed filters. However, in the latter case, the necessity of renewing or adding to the material from time to time gives an advantage to the open filters. The filters are usually dimensioned to call for supplementary filling twice a year. The kinetics of the exchange has been studied extensively by Tillmans and co-workers. Their conclusion was that the finer the material, the faster the exchange (e.g., grades of 0.5 to 1 mm, 1 to 2 mm, and 2 to 3 mm); relative exchange times are 1, 2.3, and 3.7. The exchange 1 m^3/h, quantities ranging from 200 to 250 kg $CaCO_3$ are required. The material also tends to cake, and the water to be exchanged must be appropriately prefiltered to avoid clogging of the exchange material.

Filtration on magno or neutralite

By heating dolomite at 700°C one obtains magno:

$$CaCO_3 \quad MgCO_3 \; 700° \; CaCO_3MgO + CO_2$$

A typical composition of the material is (in weight percent)

$CaCO_3$	72
MgO	22
$MgCO_3$	3
$Fe_2O_3 \cdot Al_2O_3 \quad SiO_2$	3

The magno or neutralite particles react with the CO_2 of the water 5 to 10 times quicker than does marble. The principal reaction is

$$3CO_2 + CaCO_3MgO + 2H_2O = Ca(HCO_3)_2 + Mg(HCO_3)_2$$

It has been established indeed that an analytical ration CaO/Mgo in the material is optimal in practice. THe velocity of exchange depends on the water temperature and the following empirical formula ca be handled:

$$vx = (1 + 0.085t) \times vt$$

Where v*x* and v*t* are the acceptable velocities

at temperature x and reference temperature t, generally chosen as 12°C.

The process can be operated in classical open filters of the same design as used for rapid sand filters (e.g., 1-to 1.5-m filter-medium layer). Synthetic magnos exist in regularly shaped hard materials with a head loss of about 30 cm/m and supporting backwashing by water or air and water. Another advantage of this material is that it is not influenced by the iron and manganese content of the water up to a concentration of 1 mg/L. Iron is removed simultaneously. Classical grain size is in the range 0.5 to 2 mm, but coarse grades range from 2.5 to 5 mm.

The exchange rate is directly proportional to the active surface, that is, the surface of the grains and the thickness of the active part of the filter layer. Before operation, the product is best washed to limit the hydroxide alkalinity of the water during the first periods of operation. After this stabilization phase, the reaction with CO_2 is practically stoichiometric. The necessary exchange capacity is best determined experimentally during the design.

A first approximation for design is to consider the process to be described as a mass transfer system:

$$-\frac{dC}{dt} = k \times C$$

and

$$k = \frac{\ln C_0 - \ln C}{t}$$

Where C and Co are the concentrations of dissolved CO_2. However, as the process is strongly temperature dependent, the activation energy must be considered:

$$k = K \exp\left(-\frac{A}{RT}\right)$$

where

k = velocity constant (s-1)

A = activation energy (j)

R = universal gas constant (8.31 J mo;-1 K-1)

T = absolute temperature (K)

K = steric factor (in the range of temperatures for drinking water, e.g., 5 to 25°C, *the steric factor is approximately 0.185 per degree)*

Injection of alkali

Alkali dissolved in water can neutralize aggressive CO_2. The most used products are lime and sodium hydroxide. The reactions are

The use of lime increases the hardness of the water; that of sodium hydroxide alters only the alkalinity. The process must be controlled to avoid any excess of reagent that would initiate softening or post-precipitation.

The theoretical calculation involves a step-by-step approach in which successive compositions are introduced in the equations as was done by Langelier. The entire problem is actually dealt with by computer, but the operational procedures remains very empirical. The attainment of a given pH is usually sufficient monitoring parameter confirmed by analytical determination of the aggressivity of precipitativity on solid calcium carbonate.

If lime is used, it is recommended that it be before a filtration stage. This also holds for caustic soda, but with careful dosing a clear water reservoir ensures sufficient safety against post-precipitation. Minimum hardness is necessary when water is transported by iron pipes (even protected) to the consumers. As a guideline, the total hardness should be at least around 50 ppm, preferably 120 ppm, with an equilibrium pH >7.

Index